Project Editor Nicole Reynolds
Designer James McKeag
Managing Editor Tori Kosara
Managing Art Editor Jo Connor
Senior Production Editor Jennifer Murray
Senior Production Controller Lloyd Robertson
Publisher Paula Regan
Art Director Charlotte Coulais
Managing Director Mark Searle

Written and edited for DK by Caroline Rowlands
Designed for DK by Jilly Slattery

Thanks also to Julia March for proofreading and Jennette ElNaggar for Americanizing

First American Edition, 2026
Published in the United States by DK Publishing, a division of Penguin Random House LLC
1745 Broadway, 20th Floor, New York, NY 10019

26 27 28 29 30 10 9 8 7 6 5 4 3 2 1
001–345152–Feb/2026

Crunchyroll

Published in Great Britain by Dorling Kindersley Limited
ISBN 978-0-5939-6440-8

DK books are available at special discounts when purchased in bulk for sales promotions, premiums, fund-raising, or educational use. For details, contact:
DK Publishing Special Markets,
1745 Broadway, 20th Floor, New York, NY 10019
SpecialSales@dk.com

Printed and bound in China
www.dk.com

MIX
Paper | Supporting responsible forestry
FSC™ C018179
www.fsc.org

This book was made with Forest Stewardship Council™ certified paper—one small step in DK's commitment to a sustainable future.
Learn more at **www.dk.com/uk/information/sustainability**

MY HERO ACADEMIA

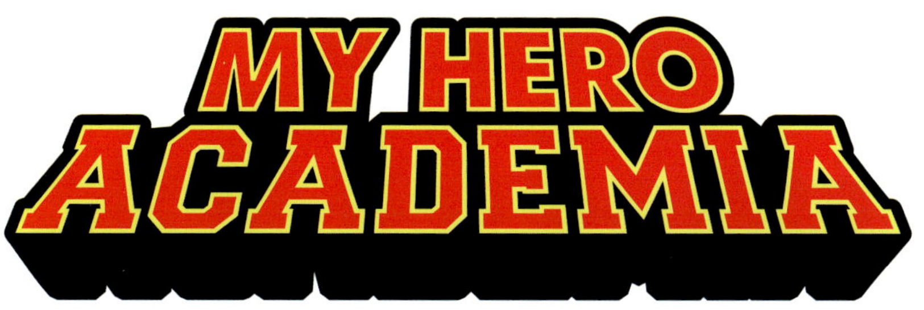

CHARACTER ENCYCLOPEDIA

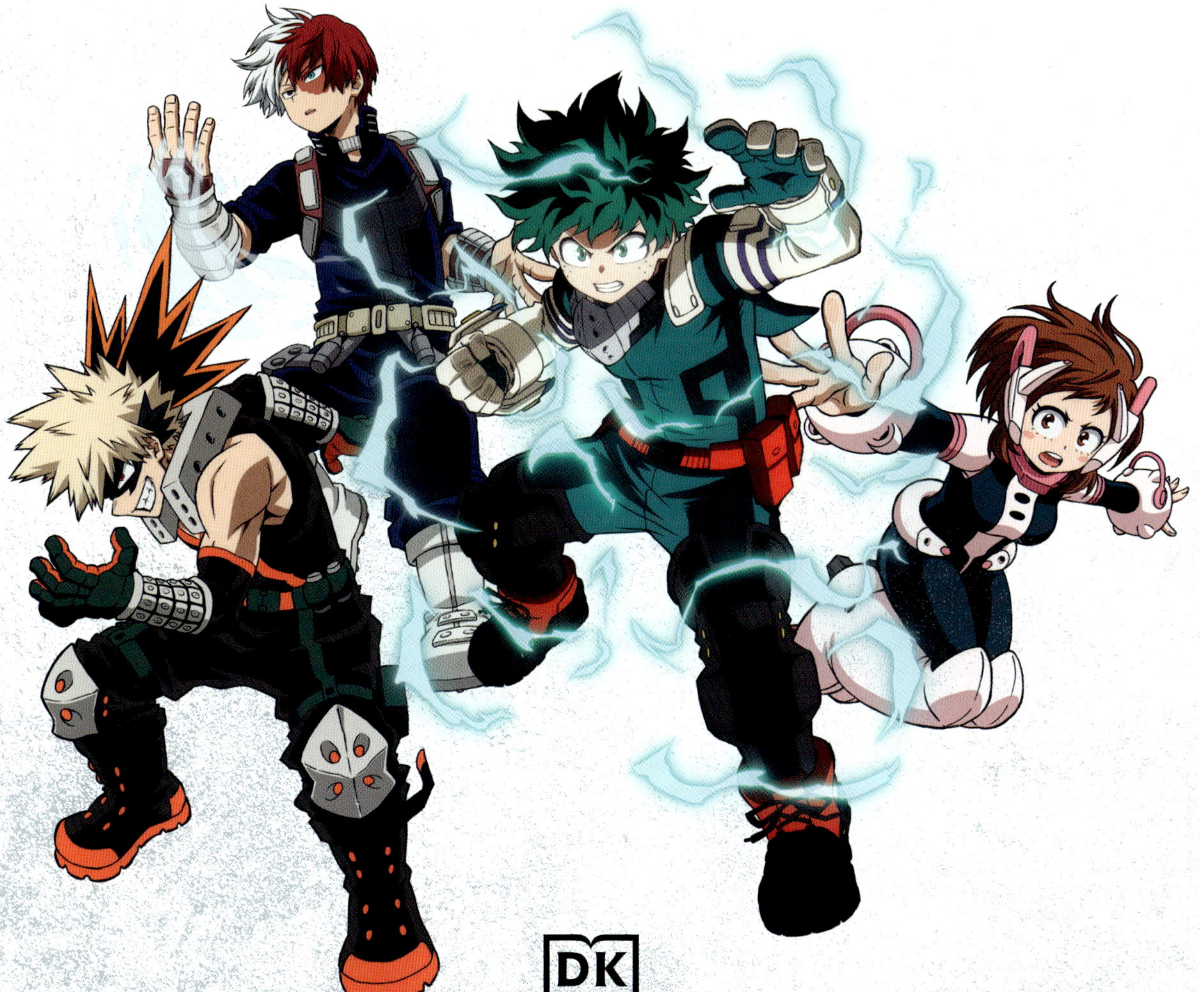

DK

CONTENTS

CLASS 1-A

HEROES IN TRAINING

CLASS 1-A

Katsuki Bakugo
Ochaco Uraraka
Shoto Todoroki
Midoriya and his classmates train hard and face endless battles as they strive to achieve their dreams of becoming Pro Heroes.

Izuku Midoriya

The heroic boy who inherited the No. 1 Pro Hero's Quirk!

Despite being born without a Quirk, Midoriya constantly demonstrates his heroism through his strong sense of justice and kindness to others. His determination and bravery impresses All Might, who passes on his One For All Quirk to Midoriya, making his dreams of becoming the greatest hero come true.

BIRTHDAY: *July 15*
HERO NAME: *Deku*
HEIGHT: *166 cm (5 ft 5 in)*
QUIRK: *One For All*
MOVE: *Delaware Smash*
QUOTE: *"Meddling in another's business is the essence of being a hero."*

Long gloves support Midoriya's arms after they were damaged in battle with Muscular

Four symmetrical freckles (in diamond formation) on each cheek

Metal soles increase his kicking power when he performs his Ultimate Move, Shoot Style

DID YOU KNOW?
One For All is a Quirk that carries the accumulated power of past users.

POWERFUL MENTOR

Midoriya is determined to make Pro Hero Sir Nighteye take him on at Nighteye Agency. He wants to prove he is worthy of his One For All Quirk.

At U.A. High School, Midoriya trains his Quirk through class activities, sports festivals, and exams with his classmates. He even comes up against the evil villains in his first year at school. By studying and training hard, Midoriya proves he's a worthy adversary and wants to do justice to the amazing All For One Quirk he has inherited from his hero, All Might.

Costume is constantly evolving to help him fight more strongly

RECKLESS DANGER

Midoriya searches for the leader of the League of Villains, Tomura Shigaraki, and All For One all night by himself. He is isolated and trapped by his strong responsibility to handle this duty alone.

DID YOU KNOW?

Midoriya inherited more Quirks from the One For All wielders, including Blackwhip and Float.

Katsuki Bakugo

An ambitious and explosive talent

Bakugo has great confidence in his abilities and his fighting style is all-out offense. The nitro-glycerin-like fluid that seeps from the sweat glands on Bakugo's palms causes explosions, which he can use to thrust himself forward rapidly.

Protective metal neck brace

Explosive grenades

Tough metal knee pads

OLD RIVALS

Initially Bakugo is hostile toward Midoriya, but they eventually learn to fight alongside each other. They team up to battle Tomura Shigaraki after he uses his Decay Quirk against Jaku City.

BIRTHDAY: *April 20*
HERO NAME: *Great Explosion Murder God Dynamight*
HEIGHT: *172 cm (5 ft 8 in)*
QUIRK: *Explosion*
MOVE: *Stun Grenade*
QUOTE: *"I guess I'm a perfectionist."*

CLASSMATES

When Midoriya goes off searching for Tomura Shigaraki and All For One alone, Bakugo fights alongside his classmates to show Midoriya he needs and has their support. He tells Midoriya that you cannot win alone, and that how you win is by saving everyone.

DID YOU KNOW?

Bakugo wants to be No. 1 Pro Hero and surpass All Might.

INTERNSHIP

Bakugo joins Midoriya and Todoroki to train at Endeavor's Hero Agency. Bakugo has previously been able to use his Explosion Quirk however he likes, but now he wants to find out about what he cannot do and discover new skills and knowledge, so he can surpass the No. 1 Pro Hero.

Ochaco Uraraka

The anti-gravity student who can make things float

Cheerful and positive, Uraraka is always willing to help out anyone who needs her assistance. Opponents foolishly underestimate Uraraka's abilities due to her bubbly and friendly personality, but she often surprises them with her strategic combat skills.

Pink headband covers her ears

Small, thick pads on fingertips activate and deactivate Uraraka's amazing Quirk

Thigh-high boots

DEFYING GRAVITY!

Uraraka can make herself float with just one touch! She uses her abilities and grappling hooks to rescue others and defeat villains.

BIRTHDAY: *December 27*
HERO NAME: *Uravity*
HEIGHT: *156 cm (5 ft 1 in)*
QUIRK: *Zero Gravity*
QUOTE : *"I'm going to become a hero."*

DID YOU KNOW?

Uraraka dreams of becoming a hero so she can help provide for her hardworking parents.

CLOSE BOND

Uraraka was the first to welcome Midoriya to U.A. High School and realize how special he was. She looks up to him but also feels protective of him.

DID YOU KNOW?

Uraraka's mentor, Hado, helps her and Asui get internships with Pro Hero Ryukyu.

While on her work study with Pro Hero Ryukyu, Uraraka works well with her classmate Asui. They combine their Quirks to create the super move Meteor Fafrotskies. Urakara raises rocks into the sky and Asui uses her tongue to smash them into some battling villains who are rampaging through the middle of the city.

EVACUATION MISSION

During the Paranormal Liberation War, the huge villain Gigantomachia rampages through Jaku City. Uraraka works with Asui and uses her Quirk to protect the residents from the falling debris.

Tenya Iida

The speedy student with big ambitions

Iida is Class rep for 1-A and hopes to follow in the heroic footsteps of his elder brother Tensei. His Engine Quirk gives him engines in his calves, which propel him along at super speeds and give him an almighty kicking power.

DID YOU KNOW?
Iida took his brother's hero name to honor him after he was injured by the villain Stain.

BIRTHDAY: *August 22*
HERO NAME: *Ingenium*
HEIGHT: *179 cm (5 ft 11 in)*
QUIRK: *Engine*
QUOTE: *"I admired my brother so I aspired to become a hero."*

ALL FIRED UP

Iida gains some valuable skills during his work studies with Pro Hero Manual, which have helped make him more flexible in combat. He is eager to try out his moves when back in class.

Iida often has a serious expression

SAVING TEAMMATES

During Joint Training with Class 1-B, Iida saves Todoroki. This training situation reminds Iida of his battle with Stain and how he let his hatred of him get in the way of rescuing those in front of him.

Iida rejects Midoriya's offer to team up for the cavalry battle in U.A. High School Sports Festival. He admires Midoriya's actions but wants to develop his own heroic abilities by challenging Midoriya as a rival.

HELPING HAND

Iida tries to keep up with Midoriya's speed to save him from fighting alone, and to bring him back to U.A. High School. He reminds Midoriya that meddling when you don't need to is the essence of being a hero.

Shoto Todoroki

The loner who commands ice and flame!

DID YOU KNOW?
When Midoriya and Bakugo eat at Todoroki's house, they learn Todoroki's favorite food is cold soba noodles.

Todoroki's amazing Quirk enables him to freeze with his right hand and burn with his left. The real scale of his power is unknown, but his ability ensures Todoroki is always top of the class at U.A. High School.

His utility belt holds medical capsules that can save lives when rescuers can't

Todoroki often leads with his ice powers

FIERY FIGHTER

During Joint Training with Class 1-B, Todoroki battles Tetsutetsu. He strives to surpass his limits by turning his incredible heat and fire power on his tough opponent.

BIRTHDAY: *January 11*
HERO NAME: *Shoto*
HEIGHT: *176 cm (5 ft 9 in)*
QUIRK: *Half-Cold Half-Hot*
QUOTE: *"Keep focused on what you want to become."*

Todoroki decides to do his internship at the agency belonging to his father, Endeavor, with Midoriya and Bakugo. They train to enhance their Quirks—and work together as a team to rescue Todoroki's brother, Natsuo, when he's kidnapped by villains.

DID YOU KNOW?

At first Todoroki preferred to use the ice part of his Quirk, because he had inherited it from his mother.

TODOROKI'S PROMISE

During the Paranormal Liberation War, Endeavor is physically and mentally injured after discovering his eldest son, Toya, is the villain Dabi. Todoroki and his family commit to face their troubled past.

Tsuyu Asui

The fearless fighter with froglike abilities

DID YOU KNOW?
Asui decided on her hero name, Rainy Season Hero Froppy, in elementary school.

Asui's Frog Quirk has given her a long, sticky tongue that can stretch to 20 m (66 ft), the ability to hop on all fours to great heights, and a super-fast swimming speed. A devoted student, Asui is never afraid to say what she thinks and always manages to stay calm and focused, even in a crisis.

BIRTHDAY: *February 12*
HERO NAME: *Froppy*
HEIGHT: *150 cm (4 ft 11 in)*
QUIRK: *Frog*
QUOTE: *"I say everything that comes to my mind."*

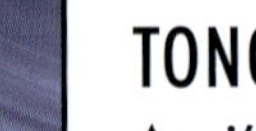

TONGUE TWISTER

Asui's tongue is a versatile tool and weapon. She uses it to reach and wrap around items (and people), whack and slap enemy opponents, and fling objects high into the air, including herself.

FROPPY HOPPER

Asui can use her froglike abilities to leap to extreme heights. When she is exposed to cold temperatures, she will go into hibernation, just like a frog.

Known for her calm and straightforward personality, Asui is also clever and resourceful. She comes up with the plan to swallow a pair of handcuffs that eventually helps her, and her Class 1-A classmate Tokoyami, to defeat Ectoplasm and pass their final exam.

CAMOUFLAGE

During her Provisional Hero License Exam, Asui uses the camouflage aspect of her Quirk. She attacks multiple villains by stealth and knocks them down with her tongue.

Asui's Quirk enables her to secrete a toxic mucus, which can sting others

Hair tied in a bow is Asui's trademark hairstyle

Minoru Mineta

Smarter than he seems and always looking for love

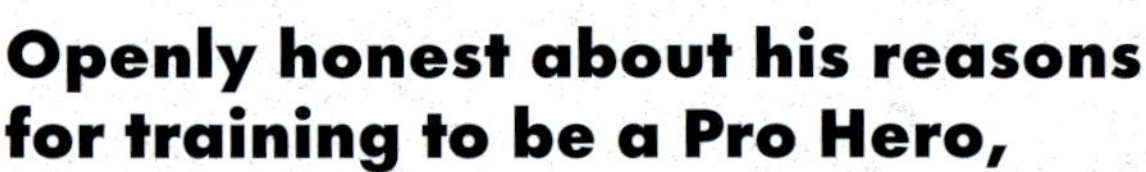

Openly honest about his reasons for training to be a Pro Hero, Mineta (aka Grape Juice) will happily admit he longs to become popular and attract girls. His Pop Off Quirk enables him to create ball-like objects from his head that stick to things and won't come off.

DID YOU KNOW?
Mineta's grape balls are extremely sticky, and strong enough to stop an enemy moving.

BIRTHDAY: *October 8*
HERO NAME: *Grape Juice*
HEIGHT: *108 cm (3 ft 6 in)*
QUIRK: *Pop Off*
QUOTE: *"Come on. Grape Rush!"*

Grape balls don't stick to Mineta

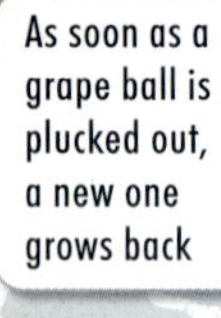

SMALL BUT MIGHTY

Mineta teams up with Asui to form a rescue squad to save a civilian during a training drill at Ground Beta.

GIGANTOMACHIA ATTACK

During the Paranormal Liberation War, Mineta teams up with Pro Heroes and his fellow students. He helps fire cannons created by Yaoyorozu at Gigantomachia, which enables Kirishima to escape.

If Mineta pulls off too many grape balls, he can bleed

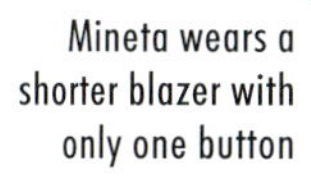

Mineta is a key part to Class 1-A's rescue mission to bring Midoriya back to U.A. High School after he leaves. When Midoriya resists his classmates' arguments for him to return, Mineta tells Midoriya that he likes him because he fought against villains, showing his courage and bravery, not because he inherited Quirks from All Might.

MINETA BEADS

When Class 1-A go after Midoriya, Mineta is flung into the air by Asui's sticky tongue. He tries to secure Midoriya with his Mineta Beads (a string of his grape balls).

DID YOU KNOW?

Mineta was part of the dance team at the U.A. High School Festival.

Eijiro Kirishima

The tough student who can turn his body into a weapon

Inspired by his favorite Pro Hero, Crimson Riot, Kirishima (aka Red Riot) is always determined to protect his friends from villains. His amazing Quirk hardens his body, making him resistant to physical attacks and able to deliver powerful strikes.

BIRTHDAY: *October 16*
HERO NAME: *Red Riot*
HEIGHT: *170 cm (5 ft 7 in)*
QUIRK: *Hardening*
QUOTE: *"As if I'd die!"*

DID YOU KNOW?

Before attending U.A. High School, Kirishima was insecure that his Quirk was not good enough for hero work.

UNBREAKABLE

Unbreakable is Kirishima's Ultimate Move. When Kirishima reaches his maximum hardening level, he is unbreakable, but he can maintain it for only 30 to 40 seconds. He uses this Ultimate Move for the first time when interning for the Pro Hero Fatgum.

A popular classmate, Kirishima has a close friendship with Bakugo. His upbeat personality helps him cope with Bakugo's abrasive and abrupt ways. He bravely joins the rescue team to save Bakugo when he is kidnapped by the villains.

Red R on belt buckle

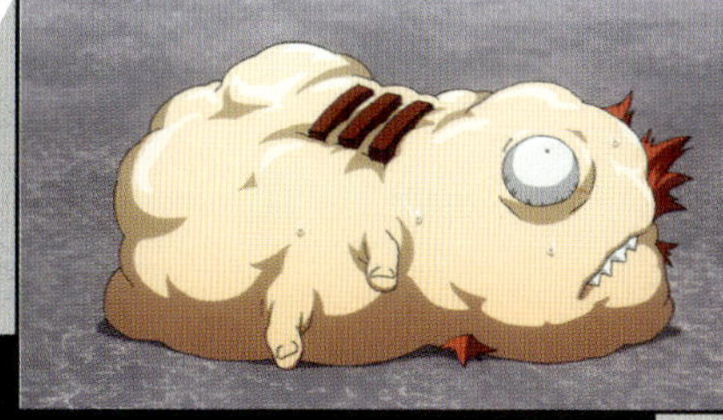

MEATBALL ATTACK

Kirishima is transformed into a lump of flesh by Shisikura (a student from Shiketsu High School) during the Provisional Hero License Exam.

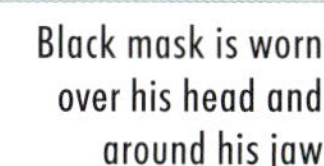

Black mask is worn over his head and around his jaw

Momo Yaoyorozu

The genius who can create anything

Clever and cooperative, Yaoyorozu quickly analyzes her classmates' strengths and weaknesses before coming up with winning strategies. She proves this by creating a version of her teacher Eraser Head's binding cloth, which she and Todoroki use to defeat him in battle during a school exam.

Using her Quirk destroys her clothes, so it's practical not to wear much

Yaoyorictionary has everything Yaoyorozu needs to know to help with her Creation Quirk

Yaoyoro-Belt

BIRTHDAY: *September 23*
HERO NAME: *Creati*
HEIGHT: *173 cm (5 ft 8 in)*
QUIRK: *Creation*
QUOTE: *"It takes time to make something big."*

CREATION QUIRK

So long as she can understand the molecular structure, Yaoyorozu can create any nonliving thing with her body. During Joint Training with Class 1-B, she creates weapons, including cannons, to battle alongside Tokoyami, Aoyama, and Hagakure.

DID YOU KNOW?

Smart Yaoyorozu figures out that Eraser Head is lying to his students about expelling whoever came last in the Quirk Apprehension Test.

Known for her strategic mind and intelligence, Yaoyorozu tries to learn from every experience. When she interns at Uwabami's office, she tries to be positive about gaining insight into the media side of hero work, even though she misses out on getting any practical hero experience. She also kindly invites her classmates to her home to help them study for the final exam.

CREATIVE STUDENT

When the Pro Hero Midnight is injured in the Gunga Mountain Villa raid, she asks Yaoyorozu to step up and help defeat the villains by putting Gigantomachia to sleep. The clever hero in training creates sedatives to help knock Gigantomachia out.

Hair pulled back into a spiky ponytail

Fumikage Tokoyami

A silent, shadowy hero

Dedicated and disciplined Tokoyami has worked hard to be able to control his powerful Quirk, Dark Shadow. The shadowy beast inside him becomes more powerful in darker surroundings, and it can grow weaker in bright light.

Cape covers Dark Shadow and helps Tokoyami to fly

Dark Shadow's enlarged arms enable Tokoyami to smash through opponents in battle

DID YOU KNOW?

Pro Hero Hawks mentors Tokoyami and teaches him crucial skills for hero work.

DANGEROUS DUO

Tokoyami trains Dark Shadow to endure bright lights ahead of the Sports Festival. He needs to train his Quirk so it can help him in any situation. He and Dark Shadow need to learn to work together as a team.

BIRTHDAY: *October 30*
HERO NAME: *Tsukuyomi*
HEIGHT: *158 cm (5 ft 2 in)*
QUIRK: *Dark Shadow*
QUOTE: *"Now when I stare into the abyss, the abyss stares back at me."*

DID YOU KNOW?

His hero name, Tsukuyomi, comes from the moon god in Japanese mythology.

During the Paranormal Liberation War, Tokoyami joins Kaminari on the front line in the fight against the villains. He hopes all the training he received with Hawks will help him on the mission. Tokoyami's Ultimate Move, Black Fallen Angel, is enabled by resting his body on Dark Shadow, who carries him through the air. His powerful Ragnarok move is strong enough to repel dangerous enemies like Re-Destro.

BRAVE RESCUE

When Dabi attacks Tokoyami during the Paranormal Liberation War, he cannot fight back as Dark Shadow is weakened by Dabi's bright flames. Tokoyami flees, heroically taking Hawks with him.

While he has a bird head, Tokoyami has a human body from the neck down

Red choker necklace

Denki Kaminari

A highly charged student with skills that shock

Kaminari uses the electricity from his body as an effective weapon against opponents in combat. His Quirk is powerful—but overusing it causes him to short-circuit, behave foolishly, and babble incoherently.

DID YOU KNOW?

Kaminari doesn't pay much attention in class and is easily distracted from studying for exams.

BIRTHDAY: *June 29*
HERO NAME: *Chargebolt*
HEIGHT: *168 cm (5 ft 6 in)*
QUIRK: *Electrification*
QUOTE: *"We've become the center of attention in just one day."*

SHOCK AND AWE

Kaminari, aka Chargebolt, learns to control his Quirk so that he can modify his wattage output.

SURPRISING SKILLS

During the Paranormal Liberation War, Kaminari's electrically powered attacks disable the villains. This enables the Pro Heroes to raid Gunga Mountain Villa (the villains' headquarters).

Hair has a messy side part with a black, lightning-shaped streak

Kaminari can shock anyone he comes into contact with

Kaminari cares about his friends and is quick to excite and encourage his classmates. He sometimes hangs out with Mineta, due to their shared interest in girls. During the U.A. High School Festival, he is impressed that his friend Jiro can play so many instruments. He compliments her on her skills and encourages Jiro to be proud of her hobby, not hide it.

DID YOU KNOW?

Mei Hatsume helps Kaminari create a Sharpshooter device to help him manipulate his Quirk.

Yuga Aoyama

Nothing can stop this sparkly twinkler

With a tendency to be overdramatic and self-centered, Aoyama is also capable of great kindness to his friends and classmates. As a child he struggled with his Quirk, Navel Laser, which often gave him a stomachache after he used it.

DID YOU KNOW?
His hero name Can't Stop Twinkling reflects his desire to always stand out.

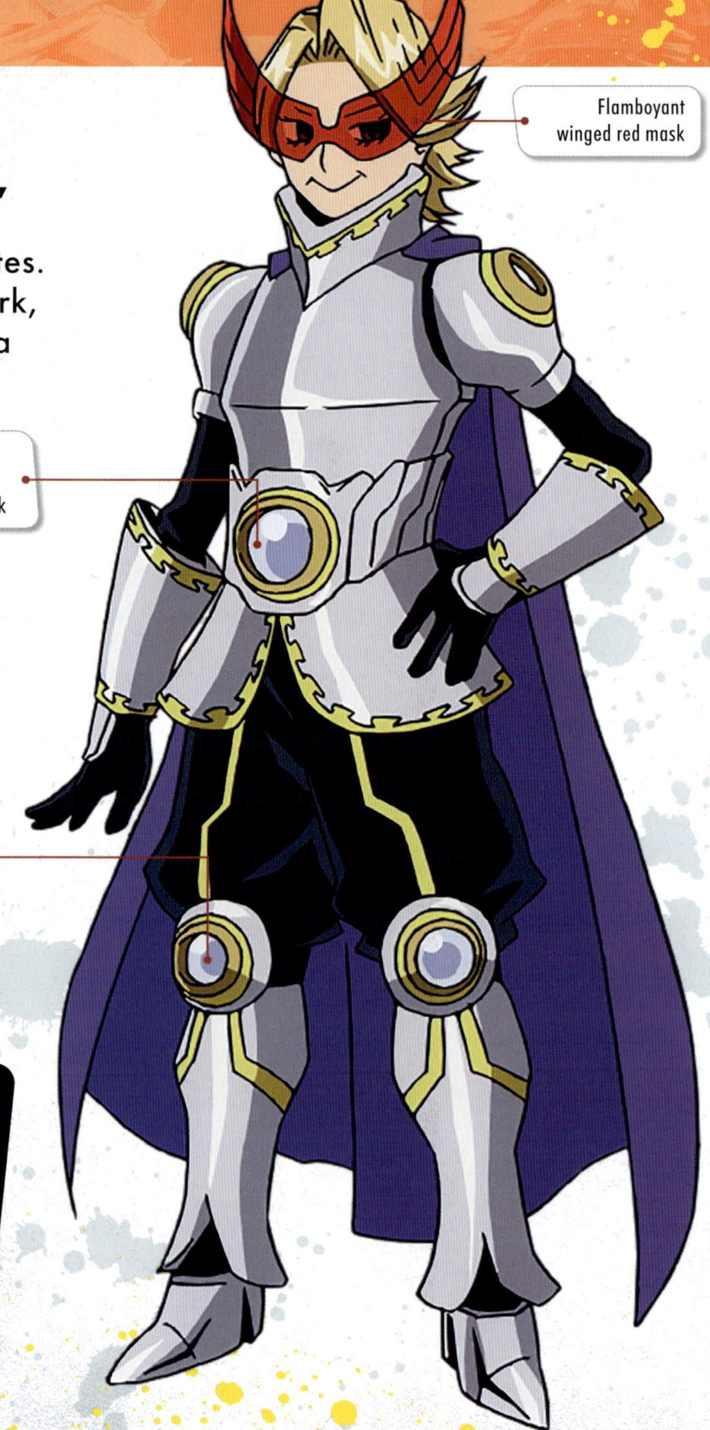

BIRTHDAY: *May 30*
HERO NAME: *Can't Stop Twinkling*
HEIGHT: *168 cm (5 ft 6 in)*
QUIRK: *Navel Laser*
QUOTE: *"I've always wanted to be an equal."*

LASER LIGHT

During the Provisional Hero License Exam, Iida encourages Aoyama to believe in himself and not to give up. Aoyama uses his Navel Laser Light to help his classmates and himself pass the exam.

Aoyama can speak French

Aoyama's signature move is Navel Buffet Laser, where he fires beams from his navel, shoulders, and knees. This move puts a lot of pressure on him, though. When he uses his Navel Saber move, Aoyama can also manipulate his laser to create a light blade, which can slice things.

BACKUP SUPPORT

During the Paranormal Liberation War Aoyama joins the villa backup team. Along with some of his classmates and students from Class 1-B, the team attempt to prevent any villains from escaping the Gunga Mountain Villa.

Kyoka Jiro

The sound specialist who attacks and supports

Jiro can turn her own heartbeat into a weapon. By channeling the sound of her heartbeat through her earphone jacks to create sonic boom attacks and vibrations, Jiro is capable of shattering objects and creating tremors.

Her earphone jacks act as extra limbs that Jiro can change the length of

BIRTHDAY: *August 1*
HERO NAME: *Earphone Jack*
HEIGHT: *154 cm (5 ft)*
QUIRK: *Earphone Jack*
QUOTE: *"A true hero makes you believe."*

Amplifiers can be slammed into the ground to create a shattering vibration

CENTER STAGE

At first Jiro tries to hide her love of music from her classmates. But encouraged by her friends, she shows her true talents at the U.A. High School Festival.

Boots with built-in stereos

DID YOU KNOW?

Jiro can also plug her earphones into walls to listen in on others.

EAR TO THE WALL

Jiro uses her Quirk to listen out for the enemy during the Joint Training Battle with Class 1-B.

When she's not playing music, Jiro is listening to it

This music-loving sound specialist is more suited to ranged combat so prefers to work with others and have a partner with her during battles. Jiro is often paired with Kaminari and battles alongside him in the Battle Trial and Unforeseen Joint Simulation training.

Jiro alternates the school uniform blazer with a waistcoat

MUSICAL TALENT

Jiro has been musical from a very young age—both her parents are musicians. They encouraged her in music but also to follow her dream of standing up for others and becoming a hero.

DID YOU KNOW?

Jiro sings and plays the bass guitar at the U.A. High School Festival.

Mina Ashido

The upbeat student with an acidic Quirk

Ashido's acid-creating Quirk enables her to secrete a corrosive acid from her body. She can cleverly control its concentration so it's effective in different ways, like making surfaces slippery or melting objects. Ashido possesses courage and dedication, but her academic performance is quite poor and she often finds herself at the bottom of the class with her test results.

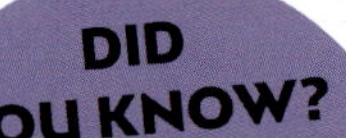

DID YOU KNOW?
While she's never fallen in love, Ashido loves romance!

SUPER SOCIAL

Ashido is highly excitable, easygoing, and loves to hang out with her friends, gossip, and go shopping. Kind and supportive, she offers to help her friends learn to dance for the Sports Festival.

Overusing her Quirk can cause Ashido 's skin to dehydrate

BIRTHDAY: *July 30*
HERO NAME: *Pinky*
HEIGHT: *159 cm (5 ft 3 in)*
QUIRK: *Acid*
QUOTE: *"With this... it's over!"*

DANCE OFF

Midoriya wants to learn some of Ashido's dance moves as he thinks they will be helpful in combat.

During Joint Training with Class 1-B, Ashido teams up with Midoriya, Uraraka, and Mineta against Monoma, Kodai, Yanagi, and Shinso. Ashido uses her move Acid Veil to create a strong acidic wall to protect her teammates when they come under attack. She fires acid bullets on her opponents with her Acid Shot move, helping her team win the battle.

Mezo Shoji

A pro at gathering intel

DID YOU KNOW?
The tentacles on his shoulders can duplicate his body parts.

Shoji is protective of his classmates and, despite his appearance, is gentle and friendly. His Dupli-Arms Quirk gives him great search and combat abilities. Shoji is willing to sacrifice himself to save others, like when he carries Midoriya on his back and saves him from Dark Shadow during Summer Training Camp.

Shoji covers his face with a mask

Eyes and ears can duplicate to his tentacles to search for villains

OCTOBLOW

Shoji has great control over his Quirk. This enables him to defend himself and his classmates with signature moves like Octoblow during training sessions and in combat with villains.

BIRTHDAY: *February 15*
HERO NAME: *Tentacole*
HEIGHT: *187 cm (6 ft 2 in)*
QUIRK: *Dupli-Arms*
QUOTE: *"I'm used to people being scared of me."*

TEAM DEFENSE

Shoji is part of the villa backup team during the Paranormal Liberation War. His mission is to provide support while the Pro Heroes raid the villains' headquarters at the Gunga Mountain Villa and defeat Gigantomachia when he is awakened.

During the Provisional Hero License Exam, Shoji shows all he has learned from interning with the Pro Hero Gang Orca. He is tasked with saving (fake) victims from a disaster site and strategically suggests to his classmates that they would be more effective splitting into small groups. He uses his Quirk to search and rescue, and passes the exam.

Mashirao Ojiro

The martial arts all-rounder

BIRTHDAY: *May 28*
HERO NAME: *Tailman*
HEIGHT: *169 cm (5 ft 7 in)*
QUIRK: *Tail*
QUOTE: *"I won't let you go."*

The powerful tail that grows from Ojiro's body can be wielded to smack enemies and to grip onto objects, so he can move with monkey-like mobility. Hardworking and dignified, Ojiro uses his Tail Quirk and knowledge of martial arts to defeat his opponents.

DID YOU KNOW?
Ojiro used his tail to run a race in the Quirk Assessment Test.

TWIRLING TAIL DANCE

Ojiro uses his Twirling Tail Dance move against Tsunotori during their Joint Training battle. He spins quickly to twist his tail and strike her remote-controlled horns.

Ojiro, aka Tailman, is a loyal and protective friend to Midoriya and joins his classmates in rescuing him, after he leaves U.A. High School. While battling with Midoriya, he manages to catch him with his powerful tail before Tokoyami captures him. Ojiro hopes to make the world a better place and put an end to despair.

Hanta Sero

A laid-back tape-wielding hero

Sero's Tape Quirk enables him to wrap up opponents from afar, keeping them all tied up and out of the action. His adhesive tape also helps him to get around, and Sero can use it to swing from point to point or escape danger.

DID YOU KNOW?
Sero sleeps through his practical exam after Midnight uses her Quirk on him.

TAPE TRAINING

At the end of the first term, Midoriya invites his classmates to train with him at the pool. Sero tries to beat his friends using his tape, but Todoroki wins the race.

BIRTHDAY: *July 28*
HERO NAME: *Cellophane*
HEIGHT: *177 cm (5 ft 8 in)*
QUIRK: *Tape*
QUOTE: *"Aw, shoot! This backfired."*

DID YOU KNOW?

As well as shooting out tape, Sero can also retract it.

Pointed fringe and hair ends

While never top of his class, Sero is strategic and tactical in battle and works well with his classmates to utilize his Quirk. His Ultimate Moves are Trident, where he uses his tape to launch objects at opponents, and Barricade Tape, where he covers his surroundings to protect himself and his allies from attack.

STICKING TOGETHER

During Joint Training, Sero teams up with Bakugo, Jiro, and Sato to battle Class 1-B. His tape is super strong and sticky, enabling him to sling his classmate Jiro around quickly and make daring rescue missions for his team.

Toru Hagakure

When she attacks... nobody sees her coming

Hagakure's Quirk renders her invisible, making her the perfect choice for stealth and undercover missions. Hagakure has also mastered the skill of refracting light that passes through her and turning it into a blinding flash to stun opponents.

Costume is nothing but a pair of gloves and footwear

TRAINING PARTNERS

Hagakure trains alongside Shoji to help improve their Quirks in Summer Training Camp. Shoji creates multiple eyes to try to seek out Hagakure, while she uses her Quirk to remain unseen.

Her shoes have been updated from lace-ups to knee-high boots

DID YOU KNOW?

Hagakure interned under Pro Hero Yoroi Musha to improve her abilities.

BIRTHDAY: *June 16*
HERO NAME: *Invisible Girl*
HEIGHT: *152 cm (5 ft)*
QUIRK: *Invisibility*
QUOTE: *"Warp Refraction! Say Cheese!"*

FESTIVE FRIENDS

Hagakure celebrates Christmas with a festive party with all her friends from Class 1-A.

More of Hagakure is visible in her school uniform than in her hero costume

Hagakure's Invisibility Quirk makes her the perfect choice to give backup support in battles, as the enemy can never see her. During a school practical exam, she remains undetected by Pro Hero Snipe while her teammate Shoji distracts him. Hagakure quickly ambushes Snipe and secures him in handcuffs to get the win and pass the exam.

MISSION MIDORIYA!

Hagakure joins her classmates on their mission to bring Midoriya back to U.A. High School. They tell their friend they want to fight alongside him and share his burden.

DID YOU KNOW?

Hagakure's move Warp Refraction can warp sunlight to stun opponents with a flash of light.

Rikido Sato

The sweet student who powers up with sugar

This ripped giant of a student relies on sugar for his energy. Just 10 grams of sugar will make him five times stronger, but only for three minutes. He uses his amplified power to smash through obstacles and defeat his enemies.

SUGAR RUSH

When Class 1-A has a training exercise at Ground Beta, Sato powers up on sugar. He uses his strength to help rescue victims from a collapsing bridge.

BIRTHDAY: *June 19*
HERO NAME: *Sugarman*
HEIGHT: *185 cm (6 ft)*
QUIRK: *Sugar Rush*
QUOTE: *"Crisis averted."*

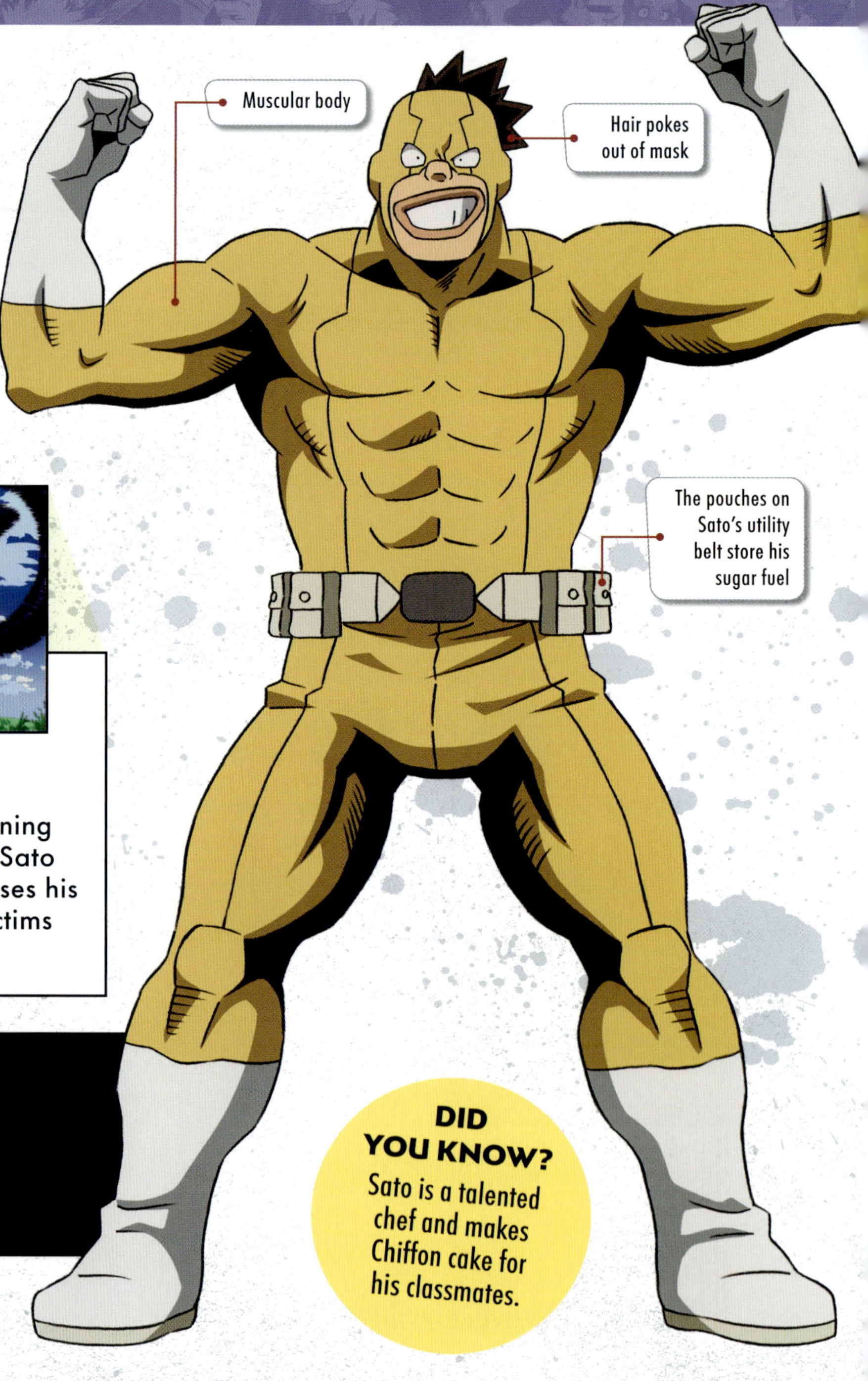

Muscular body

Hair pokes out of mask

The pouches on Sato's utility belt store his sugar fuel

DID YOU KNOW?

Sato is a talented chef and makes Chiffon cake for his classmates.

Sato is put into a team with Bakugo, Jiro, and Sero against Class 1-B's Awase, Bondo, Tokage, and Kamakiri during Joint Training. When Bakugo is imprisoned by Awase's Construction-Done-Kwik Weldcrafts super move, Sato saves him from his bonds by breaking him free with his own super move Sugar Rush.

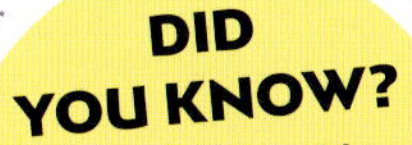

DID YOU KNOW?

Sato is trained by the No. 13 Pro Hero Shishido.

BRUTE STRENGTH

In an intense battle during the Paranormal Liberation War, Sato uses all his strength to pull a rope attached to Gigantomachia. He tries to pull open his jaw so his friends can sedate the giant.

Koji Koda

A voice that can control animals

Mask gives Koda a ducklike appearance

Koda's Quirk, Anivoice, gives him the amazing ability to communicate with animals. Whatever command he gives the animal, they will carry it out for him, from birds spying out enemy positions to swarms of bugs overwhelming his opponents.

Symbol on Koda's chest resembles an open mouth

DID YOU KNOW?
Koda may be able to communicate with animals, but he hates bugs.

HERO IN TRAINING

Koda takes part in interview training, which is conducted by Pro Hero Mt. Lady. The training aims to help students deal with all the media attention they will get when they become Pro Heroes.

Koda's ability to weaponize animals and use them for his own purpose makes him a versatile hero in training. When Class 1-A set out to return Midoriya safely to U.A. High School, Koda uses his Quirk to summon a huge flock of birds to distract Midoriya and make it difficult for him to escape.

Koda uses his large hands for sign language

Pointy, jagged, rocklike head

SILENT HERO

When Gigantomachia rampages through the city during the Paranormal Liberation War, Koda communicates with the animal kingdom and tells all the animals in the city to flee to protect themselves.

BIRTHDAY: *February 1*
HERO NAME: *Anima*
HEIGHT: *186 cm (6 ft 1 in)*
QUIRK: *Anivoice*
QUOTE: *"Bird friends, please look for damaged buildings and people in need."*

HEROES IN TRAINING

Kinoko Komori
Neito Monoma
Itsuka Kendo
The other dedicated students at U.A. High School train alongside Class 1-A, as they work to develop, and control, their amazing Quirks.

Neito Monoma

The smart-talking student who can copy Quirks

Sharp thinking and strategic, Monoma is always out to impress his fellow classmates and his rivals in Class 1-A. His useful Copy Quirk means that he can copy the Quirk of anyone he touches. During the Sports Festival, he displays his ability to think ahead and cleverly observes the Quirks of his rivals so he can beat them in later rounds.

Hair is neatly parted to the side

Monoma carries three watches

Two belts around his waist

Hero costume is smart and stylish

BIRTHDAY: *May 13*
HERO NAME: *Phantom Thief*
HEIGHT: *170 cm (5 ft 7 in)*
QUIRK: *Copy*
QUOTE: *"Come on Class 1-A. Let's see who's best once and for all!"*

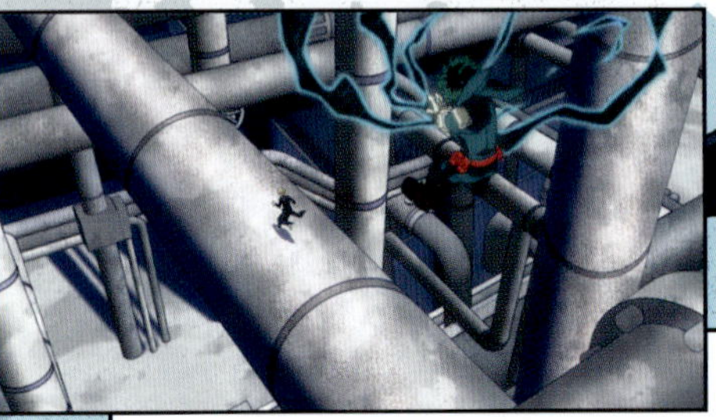

JOINT TRAINING

During Joint Training, Monoma is determined to beat Class 1-A. He deliberately provokes Midoriya, taunting him about how Bakugo is able to smile so easily when he brought an end to All Might. Midoriya reacts by unleashing his powerful Blackwhip Quirk for the first time, which he is unable to control.

DID YOU KNOW?
He can use only one copied Quirk at a time for five minutes.

Itsuka Kendo

The strong-willed class rep who packs a punch

Kendo takes care of her friends, and her no-nonsense attitude keeps her class in line. Her Big Fist Quirk enables her hands to grow big enough to grab a person and strong enough to crush metal. One punch can knock opponents out. Kendo's spirited and kind nature brings people together and makes her a good leader.

Super-sized fist when Quirk is activated

BIRTHDAY: *September 9*
HERO NAME: *Battle Fist*
HEIGHT: *166 cm (5 ft 5 in)*
QUIRK: *Big Fist*
QUOTE: *"I won't give you guys time to plan anything."*

Costume is a teal dress with a belt and black shorts under it

DID YOU KNOW?
During Summer Training, Kendo uses her Quirk to create wind power to stop a poisonous gas attack.

FIGHTING FISTS

Kendo's ability to enlarge her fists enables her to use them in different ways. During the Paranormal Liberation War, she uses their size and strength to try to restrain Gigantomachia and stop his rampaging destruction.

Tetsutetsu Tetsutetsu

The student who can turn his body into steel

The letters Fe (which stand for Iron in the Periodic Table) are stamped on the plates on Tetsutetsu's face

Hotheaded and outspoken Tetsutetsu can function in very high temperatures, thanks to being able to turn his body into metal. Even bullets cannot penetrate his skin when his Quirk is active. His brute force, durability, and enhanced strength make him a tough opponent.

BIRTHDAY: *October 16*
HERO NAME: *Real Steel*
HEIGHT: *174 cm (5 ft 9 in)*
QUIRK: *Steel*
QUOTE: *"Nothing's gonna stop my steel fist of justice."*

DID YOU KNOW?
Tetsutetsu and Tsunotori combine Quirks to create the Horn Dash Hammer move.

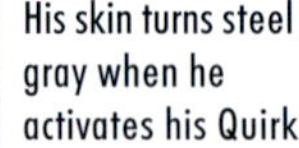

His skin turns steel gray when he activates his Quirk

MATCH 3

During Joint Training, Tetsutetsu battles Todoroki, fiercely defending himself from heat and ice attacks. Eventually both students lose consciousness and the match ends in a draw.

Ibara Shiozaki

She always takes control with her vines

Her wild green hair shoots out in all directions and can wrap up an opponent before they know what hit them. Shiozaki has great control over her Vines Quirk and can lengthen and manipulate her hair and also detach it from her head.

After using her hair in battle, she can quickly regrow it if she drinks water and absorbs sunlight

Under her white dress Shiozaki wears dark brown knee-high boots

DID YOU KNOW?
Shiozaki instantly defeats Kaminari in the Sports Festival by deflecting his power charge and trapping him in her hair.

BIRTHDAY: *September 8*
HERO NAME: *Vine*
HEIGHT: *167 cm (5 ft 6 in)*
QUIRK: *Vines*
QUOTE: *"I want to bring relief to the people."*

Juzo Honenuki

Guaranteed to stop enemies in their tracks

Protective chest plate is held in place by two thick metal shoulder straps

Strategic Honenuki wipes the floor with villains by softening the ground beneath them. One touch will soften an object, while a second one will restore it. Talented and clever, Honenuki uses his opponents' Quirks against them, such as when he softens Todoroki's ice coverage to trap him and his teammates during a Joint Training battle.

DID YOU KNOW?
Honenuki got into U.A. High School through official recommendations.

TOP TACTICS

Honenuki teams up with his classmates in the Paranormal Liberation War. He uses his Softening Quirk to make the ground unstable to trap the villains.

Plates also cover and protect his arms and legs

BIRTHDAY: *June 20*
HERO NAME: *Mudman*
HEIGHT: *174 cm (5 ft 9 in)*
QUIRK: *Softening*
QUOTE: *"I'll be taking our teammate back now."*

Shoda Nirengeki

Small and powerful, his Quirk is double the trouble

DID YOU KNOW?
He interned under Pro Hero Shishido, with Ojiro, Sato, and Shishida.

Nirengeki's Twin Impact Quirk allows him to strike once, then strike again remotely, but with significantly increased force and impact. Trustworthy and reliable in battle, Nirengeki excels at one-on-one combat and is a useful strategist to have on the team. His Quirk also enables him to enhance and strengthen the attacks carried out by his allies.

Eye-scouting device to detect opponents

BIRTHDAY: *February 2*
HERO NAME: *Mines*
HEIGHT: *165 cm (5 ft 5 in)*
QUIRK: *Twin Impact*
QUOTE: *"We've got this!"*

BIG IMPACT

Nirengeki uses his Twin Impact move as he fights alongside Monoma, Yanagi, and Kodai in their Joint Training battle against Midoriya, Uraraka, Mineta, and Ashido. Ashido uses her Acid Shot move against Nirengeki, before knocking him out with a huge punch.

Radar is connected to his eye-scouting device

Yosetsu Awase

Class 1-B's assist man who can lock down villains

Awase's Weld Quirk enables him to fuse any two objects together—even living things. His welding effectively traps opponents in place, rendering them helpless and no longer a threat. He is proud of his skills and confident in his ability.

Three-layered chest armor can also be used to shield Awase's face

DID YOU KNOW?
Awase has to be touching both objects to weld them together.

ASSIST MAN

Awase combines his stealth abilities with his Quirk to attack Bakugo in a Joint Training battle. He then uses his welding skills to make a protective suit.

Two blue bags on Awase's belt store wood and metal to help with his Quirk

BIRTHDAY: *November 7*
HERO NAME: *Welder*
HEIGHT: *172 cm (5 ft 8 in)*
QUIRK: *Weld*
QUOTE: *"My Weldcraft is... complete!"*

Kosei Tsuburaba

The student who can stop enemies with just one puff

Tsuburaba can turn the air he breathes into solid, invisible walls. He cleverly uses his Solid Air Quirk to defend against others in battle and also to trap opponents. In the Cavalry Battle Finale, during the Sports Festival, Tsuburaba creates an air shield to protect his team. But Bakugo blasts his way through to take their headbands and their points.

BIRTHDAY: *May 19*
HERO NAME: *Tsuburaba*
HEIGHT: *170 cm (5 ft 7 in)*
QUIRK: *Solid Air*
QUOTE: *"I've trained my Quirk and got a new move. Air Prison!"*

AIR ATTACK

During Joint Training, Tsuburaba traps Shinso in a box of air with his Air Prison move. He and his teammates, Shiozaki, Shishida, and Rin, are eventually defeated by Asui, Kaminari, Kirishima, and Koda.

Hero costume is a light, casual jacket

Boots with circular shapes on the soles

DID YOU KNOW?
His solidified air is soundproof, which renders his enemies unable to communicate.

Sen Kaibara

The super-spinning drill master of offense

This human drill's body parts spin at high speed and are capable of deflecting attacks and also grinding down the toughest of defensive armor. Kaibara is usually happy to go with the flow and follow the lead of others. But he is not afraid to speak his mind, like when he tells Monoma they need to keep running and try to retain their points in the Cavalry Battle Finale during the Sports Festival.

SPINNING ATTACKS

This talented student combines his Gyrate Quirk with his close-combat skills to battle Ojiro in Joint Training. Annoyingly, Iida charges in and drags him off to jail, taking him out of the fight.

Costume's spiral pattern reflects his hero name

Spiral gloves act like drills

DID YOU KNOW?
Kaibara's Quirk makes him good at offense and defense in Joint Training.

BIRTHDAY: *June 12*
HERO NAME: *Spiral*
HEIGHT: *172 cm (5 ft 8 in)*
QUIRK: *Gyrate*
QUOTE: *"Gotcha now!"*

Reiko Yanagi

The spooky student with telekinetic powers

Yanagi's Poltergeist Quirk allows her to manipulate and move objects with the power of her mind. When in battle, nearby objects can become her weapons. She can even move multiple objects at the same time, so long as they don't weigh more than a human.

BIRTHDAY: *February 11*
HERO NAME: *Emily*
HEIGHT: *165 cm (5 ft 5 in)*
QUIRK: *Poltergeist*
QUOTE: *"But looking at the fight right now, don't you think Midoriya's spooky?"*

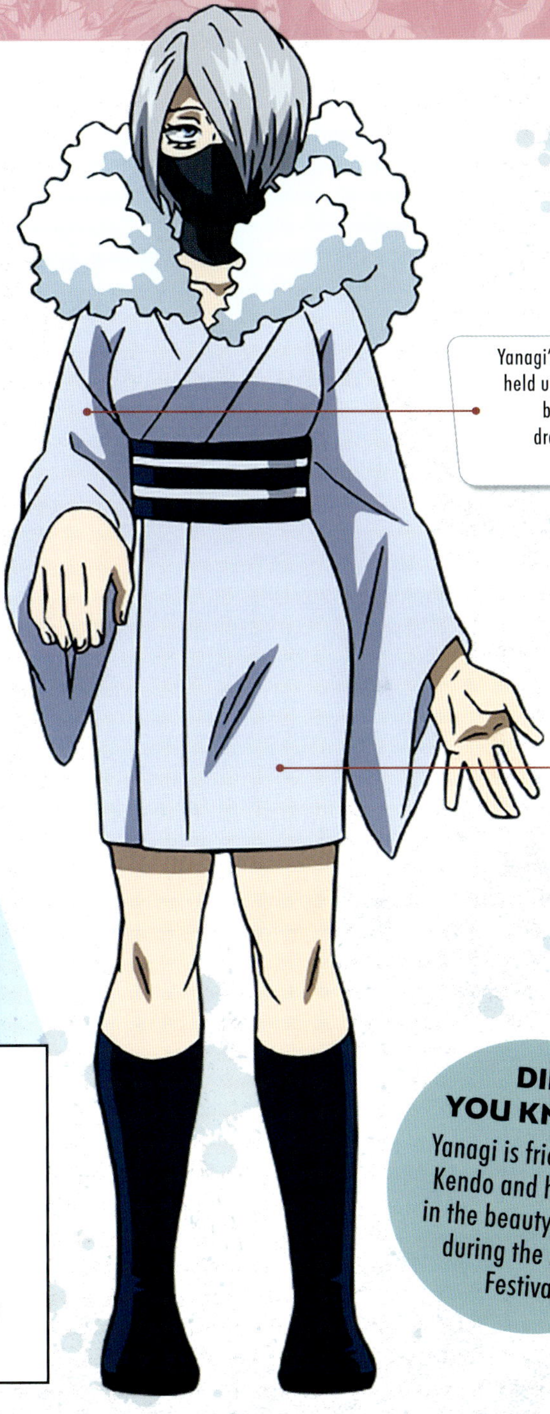

MYSTERIOUS GIRL

Yanagi utilizes her Quirk's impact by combining it with the Quirks of others. When battling Class 1-A, Kodai enlarges objects, which Yanagi then sends flying at the opponents.

Yanagi's arms are usually held up, with her elbows bent and her hands draped down… a bit like a zombie

Lilac kimono with fur trim

DID YOU KNOW?
Yanagi is friends with Kendo and helps her in the beauty pageant during the School Festival.

Jurota Shishida

The teen beast who dominates with pure power

Intelligent and refined as a student, Shishida becomes wild and reckless when his Beast Quirk is activated. His physical strength and combat skills increase with his Quirk, making him difficult to beat or defend against when he is in his dangerous mauling-attack mode.

DID YOU KNOW? Shishida has a role in the play Class 1-B perform in the School Festival.

ENHANCED ABILITIES

When his Quirk is activated, Shishida has super speed, strength, and enhanced senses, which all help him make surprise attacks. He uses his Roaring Rage move on Kaminari and Koda during the first round of Joint Training.

BIRTHDAY: *March 26*
HERO NAME: *Gevaudan*
HEIGHT: *174 cm (5 ft 9 in)*
QUIRK: *Beast*
QUOTE: *"Roaring Rage."*

Yui Kodai

The size changer who can shrink and grow objects

What she lacks in combat ability Kodai makes up for with the support she gives with her useful Quirk. She can change the size of any nonliving thing, and this versatile ability can see her create giant weapons for her allies or blindside enemies by suddenly throwing up a giant wall. A simple tap of her fingers together then restores everything to its normal size.

DID YOU KNOW?
Kodai always remains calm during battle.

BIRTHDAY: *December 19*
HERO NAME: *Rule*
HEIGHT: *160 cm (5 ft 3 in)*
QUIRK: *Size*
QUOTE: *"Now release."*

SIZE MATTERS

Kodai uses her Quirk to enlarge any object on hand, like this giant screw, to attack Mineta with during their Joint Training battle.

Hiryu Rin

The kung fu student with scales

The scales on Rin's body can be used as a coat of armor or fired off like bullets to attack opponents. He excels at close-range combat but can swiftly switch to a long-range attack, thanks to the versatility of his Scales Quirk.

Visor on Rin's head has small slits to see through

Belt with three pouches

Scale gauntlets enable Rin to fire off his scales at long range

BIRTHDAY: *July 14*
HERO NAME: *Long Weizi*
HEIGHT: *170 cm (5 ft 7 in)*
QUIRK: *Scales*
QUOTE: *"You really move well."*

UNDER PRESSURE

Hiryu teams up with Shiozaki, Tsuburaba, and Shishida in the Joint Training battle against Class 1-A. He is defeated by Asui and ends up imprisoned.

DID YOU KNOW?
Rin is an international student from China.

Kinoko Komori

Curious and creative with her airborne attacks

Komori's Mushroom Quirk enables her to spread dangerous spores quickly and effectively to defeat her opponents. These spores grow quickly into mushrooms that can overwhelm her enemies or provide useful ground cover for her allies to hide in.

BIRTHDAY: *December 2*
HERO NAME: *She-Mage*
HEIGHT: *152 cm (5 ft)*
QUIRK: *Mushroom*
QUOTE: *"Cute little mushrooms for everybody."*

Brown belt holds her shroom shooters

Polka-dot hero costume is inspired by Komori's love of mushrooms

SHROOMTASTIC

The mischief-making Komori teams up with Kendo, Kuroiro, and Fukidashi to battle Hagakure, Tokoyami, and Yaoyorozu in the second round of Joint Training. She loves to pepper her speech with shroomy language and mushroom quips as she spawns mushrooms. Her amazing skills help secure Class 1-B a win.

DID YOU KNOW?

Komori's spores will spread more quickly in a humid environment.

Togaru Kamakiri

This razor-sharp hero is ready to fight

Hotblooded and aggressive, Kamakiri is all about carving. Full of bravado, he loves to boast of tearing his opponents to shreds with his Razor Sharp Quirk. When he activates his Quirk, sharp blades emerge from his body, which he can use to carve and shred anything to pieces.

Hair styled in a green mohawk

Razor blades come out of his body

Three-toe boots

RAZOR RAGE

Kamakiri battles hard but is eventually defeated by Bakugo's raw power in his Joint Training battle against Class 1-A.

DID YOU KNOW?
Kamakiri's blades are sharp and strong enough to cut through metal.

BIRTHDAY: *January 7*
HERO NAME: *Jack Mantis*
HEIGHT: *189 cm (6 ft 2 in)*
QUIRK: *Razor Sharp*
QUOTE: *"Let's just slash 'em all to pieces."*

Pony Tsunotori

Her versatile horns lead her charging into attack

Tsunotori's Horn Cannon Quirk allows her to use her multipurpose horns to great effect. She can use them to lift and toss opponents and launch them at the enemy like a spear or dagger. She can even levitate them, then use them to help her fly through the air quickly or propel others along.

Lead rope around her head

DID YOU KNOW?
Born in the US, she speaks mixed Japanese and English.

Hero costume is horse themed, with stirrup and harness accessories

BIRTHDAY: *April 21*
HERO NAME: *Rocketty*
HEIGHT: *155 cm (5 ft 1 in)*
QUIRK: *Horn Cannon*
QUOTE: *"With the power of these four horns."*

Horseshoes on soles

RENEWABLE WEAPONS

No sooner does Tsunotori fire off her horns than new ones instantly grow back. She can remotely control four horns at a time, as she does in the Joint Training battle against Class 1-A.

Setsuna Tokage

The smart, sharp, split-apart student

DID YOU KNOW?
When Tokage is split into different parts, she can levitate in the air.

One of the most talented students in class 1-B, Tokage's Lizard Tail Splitter Quirk enables her to chip-chop her body up into multiple parts, which always confounds her opponents. The regeneration ability of Tokage's Quirk can leave her exhausted, though, so she prefers to recall her body parts rather than regenerate them, to conserve her energy.

Three-piece wrist guards protect Tokage's wrists

Black fingerless gloves with a purple panel

BIRTHDAY: *October 13*
HERO NAME: *Lizardy*
HEIGHT: *158 cm (5 ft 2 in)*
QUIRK: *Lizard Tail Splitter*
QUOTE: *"Nice. That's checkmate."*

DARING RESCUE

Tokage flies in to save Kirishima after he manages to sedate Gigantomachia during the Paranormal Liberation War.

Manga Fukidashi

An expressive student who likes to draw

Fukidashi creates speech bubbles with onomatopoeia that can conjure up the effects his words sound like. This inventive Quirk makes him a useful attacker, defender, and supporter in combat. The ability to literally turn the words he speaks into reality means his head is forever changing size, so his height and shape vary.

CREATIVE COMBAT

During a Joint Training battle against Class 1-A, Fukidashi is creative and innovative in combat. When Hagakure attacks, he's saved by Kendo and they go on to triumphantly win the round.

DID YOU KNOW?
Overuse of his Quirk can give Fukidashi a painful sore throat.

BIRTHDAY: *February 2*
HERO NAME: *Comicman*
HEIGHT: *140 cm (4 ft 7 in)*
QUIRK: *Comic*
QUOTE: *"I'm killing it today."*

Mirio Togata

The ultra-positive most powerful student

U.A. High School's most powerful student is looked up to and respected, thanks to his positive attitude, bravery, and immense fighting ability. By activating his Quirk, Permeation, Togata can phase through solid matter and people. He chooses the name Lemillion as he wants to become a hero who will save one million people, even though he cannot save everyone.

DID YOU KNOW?
Togata interns at Sir Nighteye's Agency.

BIRTHDAY: *July 15*
HERO NAME: *Lemillion*
HEIGHT: *181 cm (5 ft 11 in)*
QUIRK: *Permeation*
QUOTE: *"I become your hero."*

The 1000000 stamped on his chest reflects his hero name

THE BIG THREE

Togata first meets Midoriya when he permeates through a wall near the school dormitory. Surprised by his sudden appearance, Midoriya is impressed when Togata is later introduced to Class 1-A, along with Tamaki Amajiki and Nejire Hado, as one of The Big Three—the top three students at U.A. High School.

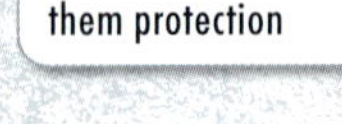

Mirio wraps his cape around others to offer them protection

Tamaki Amajiki

He reproduces the characteristics of the things he eats

Amajiki has a Quirk called Manifest, which enables him to create the physical characteristics of anything he has eaten. While interning at Fatgum's agency, he captures some thieves with octopus-tentacle arms, a crab-claw hand, and chicken legs. Fatgum praises him for using his Quirk well—even better than some Pro Heroes.

QUIET BUT DEADLY

Shy and introverted, Amajiki's trademark move is to hide his face when he feels bad about things. He is most comfortable with his classmates Togata and Hado, who both offer him lots of support.

DID YOU KNOW?
Amajiki learns a lot from his mentor, Fatgum, but doesn't like his teasing.

Purple vest stores his food supplies

Amajiki goes barefoot in his hero costume

BIRTHDAY: *March 4*
HERO NAME: *Suneater*
HEIGHT: *177 cm (5 ft 10 in)*
QUIRK: *Manifest*
QUOTE: *"I can deal with these three."*

Nejire Hado

The talkative student who sends shock waves

Hado's Quirk enables her to release powerful spiral shock waves, which she uses in close-range combat. While interning with the Pro Hero Ryukyu, she battles impressively against Shie Hassaikai gang member Rikiya Katsukame. She uses her Quirk to provide blasts of protection for herself and fellow interns Asui and Uraraka.

Straps on her arms match those around her ankles

Long, flowing lilac hair with corkscrew curls

DID YOU KNOW?
Hado won a beauty contest in the U.A. High School Festival.

CURIOUS AND CURIOUSER

Hado will blurt out whatever pops into her head and is forever asking questions in her relentless quest to know everything. She enjoys sharing her knowledge with younger students and teaching them about hero internships.

BIRTHDAY: October 6
HERO NAME: Nejire-Chan
HEIGHT: 164 cm (5 ft 5 in)
QUIRK: Surge
QUOTE: *"Full charge output."*

Hitoshi Shinso

Determined to change course and his destiny

Originally a student in Class 1-C, Shinso requests to transfer from the General Studies Course to the Hero Course. Above all else, he wants to prove himself to everyone who doubted his Brainwashing Quirk could be used for good and to become a Pro Hero that protects society.

Mask on Shinso's mouth is known as Persona Chords

BIRTHDAY: *July 1*
HEIGHT: *177 cm (5 ft 10 in)*
QUIRK: *Brainwashing*
QUOTE: *"One day I will become a proper hero and use my Quirk to help others."*

DID YOU KNOW?
Shinso was defeated by Midoriya at the first tournament match in the U.A. High School Sports Festival.

The binding cloth around Shinso's neck is the same as worn by Eraser Head, who trained him

MIND OVER MATTER

Shinso trains hard and learns capturing and battle techniques from Eraser Head. He showcases his new skills in the Joint Training battles with Class 1-A and 1-B, proving himself an effective and capable ally and teammate.

Mei Hatsume

U.A. High School's greatest inventor

Steampunk goggles are Hatsume's own invention

DID YOU KNOW?
Hatsume regards her inventions as her babies.

Hatsume is a talented and innovative student enrolled on the Support Course at U.A. High School. Direct and shameless when it comes to promoting her inventions, she is confident in the contribution her creations make to the hero industry. Hatsume's Zoom Quirk enables her to see up to 5 km (3 miles) away.

Utility belt holds a variety of tools

Speed-assisting boots

COOL CREATIONS

Hatsume creates all kinds of costumes, tools, and gadgets for her fellow students, to help support them in their training and battles. Her creative energy is boundless.

BIRTHDAY: *April 18*
HEIGHT: *157 cm (5 ft 2 in)*
QUIRK: *Zoom*
QUOTE: *"A good designer meets the reckless, ignorant, and ill-advised demands of the client."*

Inasa Yoarashi

The passionate and intense student

Yoarashi is a student in Shiketsu High, another prestigious hero school in Japan, where students train to become top heroes. He took the Provisional Hero License Exam and fought with Todoroki against Gang Orca using his strong Whirlwind Quirk, which enables him to fly.

Long cloak buttoned at the front

LICENSED TO PROTECT

After winning over the hearts and trust of the unruly kids from Masegaki Elementary School, Yoarashi finally gains his Provisional Hero License.

BIRTHDAY: *September 26*
HERO NAME: *Gale Force*
HEIGHT: *190 cm (6 ft 3 in)*
QUIRK: *Whirlwind*
QUOTE: *"Rescue exercises pump me up."*

Large glove with air pipes

Camie Utsushimi

Her illusions confound her enemies

Utsushimi's Glamour Quirk enables her to emit a smokelike substance from her mouth, which conjures up an illusion. Her creations can cover large areas but last only a short time. Her Doppelviber move, which creates the illusion of another individual, never fails to confuse.

She wears a school regulation hat that's part of the Shiketsu High School uniform with her hero costume

Metal-plated neck collar

Costume is an all-in-one jumpsuit with a zip down the front

DO-OVER

After being put to sleep by the League of Villains during the Provisional Hero License Exam, Utsushimi has to retake the exam and trains with Gang Orca.

DID YOU KNOW?

Utsushimi's use of gal languages often makes her conversation a bit confusing.

BIRTHDAY: *August 15*
HERO NAME: *Illus-O-Camie*
HEIGHT: *161 cm (5 ft 3 in)*
QUIRK: *Glamour*
QUOTE: *"Sorry hun, just a little illusion for you."*

Seiji Shishikura

Makes mincemeat of his enemies

A high-collar coat

Hero costume has a long, black apron

Seiji Shishikura believes in his school's values of obligation and respect. His Meatball Quirk gives him the ability to manipulate his opponents' bodies into raw lumps of flesh, which are unable to move and powerless in battle. He can also detach his own flesh to use as a weapon in combat.

DID YOU KNOW?
Shishikura's father is a guard at the notorious Tartarus prison.

BIRTHDAY: *February 9*
HERO NAME: *Sishikross*
HEIGHT: *172 cm (5 ft 8 in)*
QUIRK: *Meatball*
QUOTE: *"This is a demonstration."*

SHORT FUSE

Shishikura is often annoyed by Utsushimi, because she never takes things as seriously as he does.

Nagamasa Moura

The class rep who leads by example

His Extend-o-Hair Quirk enables him to control and extend the hair that grows all over his body. Wrapping opponents is easy work for this furry hero in training. Moura cares deeply about the reputation of his school, Shiketsu High, and wants to keep a good relationship between his school and U.A. High School.

DID YOU KNOW?
Moura is a class rep of Class 2-1 at Shiketsu High.

Eyes peek through hair

Costume is a pair of pants, a belt, and the school hat, leaving most of his hair exposed

MOURA'S QUIRK

Moura uses his Extend-o-Hair Quirk when in battle with the competing students in the Provisional Hero License Exam.

BIRTHDAY: *November 13*
HERO NAME: *Chewyee*
HEIGHT: *180 cm (5 ft 11 in)*
QUIRK: *Extend-o-Hair*
QUOTE: *"I'd like to build a good relationship between our schools."*

Eri

The young girl who can turn back time

Eri's powerful Rewind Quirk changes the lives of all around her. Overhaul, the head of the designated villain group known as the Shie Hassaikai, wants to use Eri's Quirk to create a drug to destroy all Quirks. He keeps her trapped underground. When Eri meets Midoriya and Togata on the street, Midoriya suspects Eri is being abused and Midoriya and Togata fight Overhaul to rescue Eri and save her from further suffering.

DID YOU KNOW?
The power source of Eri's Quirk is located in her horn.

HEROIC HEALER

Eri uses her Rewind Quirk to restore Togata's Permeation Quirk, enabling him to fight in the Paranormal Liberation War.

BIRTHDAY: *December 12*
HERO NAME: *Undecided*
HEIGHT: *110 cm (3 ft 7 in)*
QUIRK: *Rewind*
QUOTE: *"Don't be sorry, that's why I've been practicing."*

PRO HEROES

Mirko
Edge Shot
Gran Torino
On a mission to protect society and ensure world peace, the Pro Heroes are inspiring mentors to the next generation of heroes.

Endeavor

The flame hero who became No. 1 in Japan

His face is covered with a fiery mask

His scar is from a High End Nomu battle in Kyushu

With a body cloaked in burning flames, Endeavor roars into action when people need protecting. His Hellflame Quirk enables him to manipulate ferocious flames and use them to attack or move at super speed. He puts his hero work above all else, which leads to him becoming estranged from his family.

BIRTHDAY: *August 8*
HERO NAME: *Endeavor*
HEIGHT: *195 cm (6 ft 5 in)*
QUIRK: *Hellflame*
QUOTE: *"I want to be strongest."*

BURNING AMBITION

Endeavor fights alongside Midoriya and Bakugo in the Paranormal Liberation War. He uses his Prominence Burn move to defeat Shigiraki.

Endeavor's boots appear to be all burning flames

DID YOU KNOW?
His intelligence has seen him solve the most criminal cases in history.

Hawks

A hawklike Pro Hero who flies into danger

Hawk's Fierce Wings Quirk enables him to control the huge wings on his back so he can fly and also fire feathers as weapons. He is skilled in high-speed combat. If he loses all of his feathers in battle, though, it can take them up to two days to grow back.

BIRTHDAY: *December 28*
HERO NAME: *Hawks*
HEIGHT: *172 cm (5 ft 8 in)*
QUIRK: *Fierce Wings*
QUOTE: *"Is this heat the best you can do?"*

FLYING SOLO

Hawks goes undercover to spy on the League of Villains and Meta Liberation Army. He warns the Pro Heroes of the threat of their alliance.

DID YOU KNOW?
Hawks fakes Pro Hero Best Jeanist's death to earn the villain Dabi's trust.

Best Jeanist

Can control villains by just a single thread

Best Jeanist is the best-dressed Pro Hero out there. Looks matter to him, and he strongly believes that those in the limelight owe it to society to always look good and maintain a sharp and stylish physical appearance. His Quirk enables him to control the fibers of his own clothes, and those of others, and to manipulate them to do what he wants.

DID YOU KNOW?
Best Jeanist also works as a successful model alongside being No. 3 Pro Hero.

THE PUPPET MASTER

Best Jeanist has amazing control over his Fiber Master Quirk. He uses it to capture all the lieutenants of the Paranormal Liberation Front, including Tomura Shigaraki.

BIRTHDAY: *October 5*
HERO NAME: *Best Jeanist*
HEIGHT: *190 cm (6 ft 3 in)*
QUIRK: *Fiber Master*
QUOTE: *"Correcting ones like you is part of my hero activity."*

Edge Shot

Can fold his body like a piece of paper

The ability to flatten and fold his body means Edge Shot can manipulate it into any shape he wants and fit into anything he wants. This talented Pro Hero mostly uses his Quirk to strike quickly for a surprise attack, often folding himself into a blade shape to pierce the body of an opponent. His Ninpo: Thousand Sheet Pierce move enables him to pierce his enemy's skin before cutting off their blood supply.

***BIRTHDAY:** February 22*
***HERO NAME:** Edge Shot*
***HEIGHT:** 170 cm (5 ft 7 in)*
***QUIRK:** Foldabody*
***QUOTE:** "This man is a nuisance. I'll have him sleep."*

His gray locks are folded into sharp points, creating origami-style hair

Edge Shot's costume resembles that of a traditional Ninja

STEALTH MODE

Edge Shot pretends to be a pizza delivery man to distract the League of Villains when raiding their headquarters to rescue Bakugo.

DID YOU KNOW?
His Ninja-style moves have helped earn him the No. 4 Pro Hero spot.

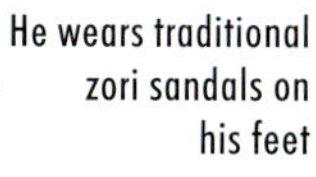
He wears traditional zori sandals on his feet

Mirko

Lives and fights like there is no tomorrow

Long, white rabbit ears blend in with her long, white hair

Miro also has a small white bobtail, just like a rabbit

Thigh-high purple stockings cover her muscular legs

Fiercely independent and brave, Mirko prefers to work alone and never backs down from a fight. Her Rabbit Quirk gives her capabilities similar to those of a rabbit. Mirko's super strength, especially in her legs, gives her a powerful, thumping kick. She is ranked No 5. in the Japanese Hero Billboard Chart.

MULTITASKER

During the Paranormal Liberation War, Mirko uses her rabbit senses to locate All For One's doctor, Kyudai Garaki, inside the hospital. Her powerful moves enable her to fight several Nomu at once, and she uses her strong legs to kick them into submission.

DID YOU KNOW?
Mirko can destroy the ground beneath her with just one thump of her powerful leg.

BIRTHDAY: *March 1*
HERO NAME: *Mirko*
HEIGHT: *159 cm (5 ft 3 in)*
QUIRK: *Rabbit*
QUOTE: *"That is not good. This can't be let loose! No matter what."*

Gran Torino

A veteran Pro Hero who shares his wisdom and skills

Gran Torino's Jet Quirk enables him to blast out jets of air from holes in the soles of his feet. It also gives him tremendous speed, a powerful kick, and the ability to propel himself through the air. When All Might passes his Quirk on to Midoriya, Gran Torino helps train the young hero in training, sharing all his knowledge.

DID YOU KNOW?
He taught All Might how to use his Quirk in combat.

His dark mask is shaped like two diamonds

His belt has a letter G monogram on it

A long cloak trails behind him

QUIRK PROTECTION

Gran Torino warns Midoriya and Bakugo that Tomura Shigaraki's Decay Quirk is more powerful than ever when he attacks Jaku City. He could steal Midoriya's One For All Quirk, which would be devastating.

BIRTHDAY: *January 28*
HERO NAME: *Gran Torino*
HEIGHT: *120 cm (3 ft 11 in)*
QUIRK: *Jet*
QUOTE: *"Do you understand? You have nowhere to run!"*

Burnin

Has hair she can turn into blistering flame throwers

Burnin's Blazing Hair Quirk enables her to pull chunks of her flaming hair off her head and throw it at enemies. As sidekick to Endeavor, she is constantly on the front line. She never hesitates to follow him into danger to bravely battle villains and protect civilians.

Silver, screwlike buttons

Fire extinguisher

SUPER SIDEKICK

Burnin tells Midoriya, Bakugo, and Todoroki that Endeavor only wants to train Todoroki when they start working at the agency, but that the sidekicks will take good care of them.

DID YOU KNOW?
Burnin is also a member of the Flaming Sidekickers group.

BIRTHDAY: *January 18*
HERO NAME: *Burnin*
HEIGHT: *169 cm (5 ft 7 in)*
QUIRK: *Blazing Hair*
QUOTE: *"Don't really need to start a fire under them, do I?"*

Mt. Lady

The statuesque Pro Hero who towers above the rest

This glamorous-looking Pro Hero loves the fame and attention her job brings her but also takes her hero responsibilities seriously. Mt. Lady's Gigantification Quirk allows her to grow to an enormous size. She can only be her normal size or her enlarged size, though. There is nothing in between.

SKYSCRAPING STRENGTH

Mt. Lady does her best to stop Gigantomachia's rampage of destruction during the Villa Raid, but she is no match for his strength.

Her purple mask has matching horns on either side

The v-shape band on her outfit matches that on her thigh-high boots and gloves

***BIRTHDAY:** August 11*
***HERO NAME:** Mt. Lady*
***HEIGHT:** 162 to 2,062 cm (5 ft 4 in to 67 ft 8 in)*
***QUIRK:** Gigantification*
***QUOTE:** "The important part of a hero activity is to know how to spend your free time."*

DID YOU KNOW?
Her move Canyon Cannon sees her deliver a flying kick while at full height.

Kamui Woods

Can capture multiple villains with his treelike tentacles

Kamui Wood's Arbor Quirk enables him to enlarge and grow his wooden body parts and turn them into branches. His branches are long and strong and can quickly capture and trap enemies. His mastery of his Quirk has seen him rise to Pro Hero No. 7 on the Japanese Hero Billboard Chart.

DID YOU KNOW?
He teams up with Mt. Lady and Edge Shot to form a group called The Lurkers.

BIRTHDAY: *May 20*
HERO NAME: *Kamui Woods*
HEIGHT: *168 cm (5 ft 6 in)*
QUIRK: *Arbor*
QUOTE: *"Preemptive Binding!"*

A small bunch of roses hangs from his belt

Hero costume has wooden kneepads, belt, and boots

BRANCHING OUT

Kamui Woods uses his branches and his signature move, Lacquered Chain Prison, to trap opponents during the Paranormal Liberation War. He also uses his branches to fling enemies and himself around.

Sir Nighteye

A brilliant brain and calm under pressure

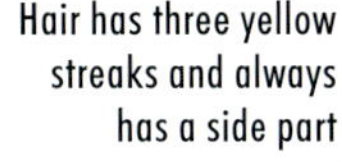

His hero costume is unusually understated and more suitable for office work

Sir Nighteye was former sidekick to All Might before moving up to be a Pro Hero. He also has his own hero agency. His Foresight Quirk enables him to see someone's future just by touching them and looking into their eyes. He is often fearful of using his Quirk and what he will see. But when he meets Midoriya, his vision for the future is off for the first time.

HEIR APPARENT

At first Sir Nighteye doesn't agree with All Might's choice of Midoriya to inherit his Quirk. He believes Togata to be the natural choice for All Might's heir.

DID YOU KNOW?

Sir Nighteye thinks a society without energy and humor is a hopeless one.

BIRTHDAY: *January 2*
HERO NAME: *Sir Nighteye*
HEIGHT: *200 cm (6 ft 7 in)*
QUIRK: *Foresight*
QUOTE: *"For the sake of the peace you wish for, you should retire as a legend."*

Fatgum

His fat absorbs attacks and then he counterattacks

Friendly, playful, and always hungry, this Pro Hero eats a lot. His Fat Absorption Quirk and large physique enable him to use his body to restrain opponents and also act as a shield to protect others. He is a supportive mentor to students Amajiki and Kirishima.

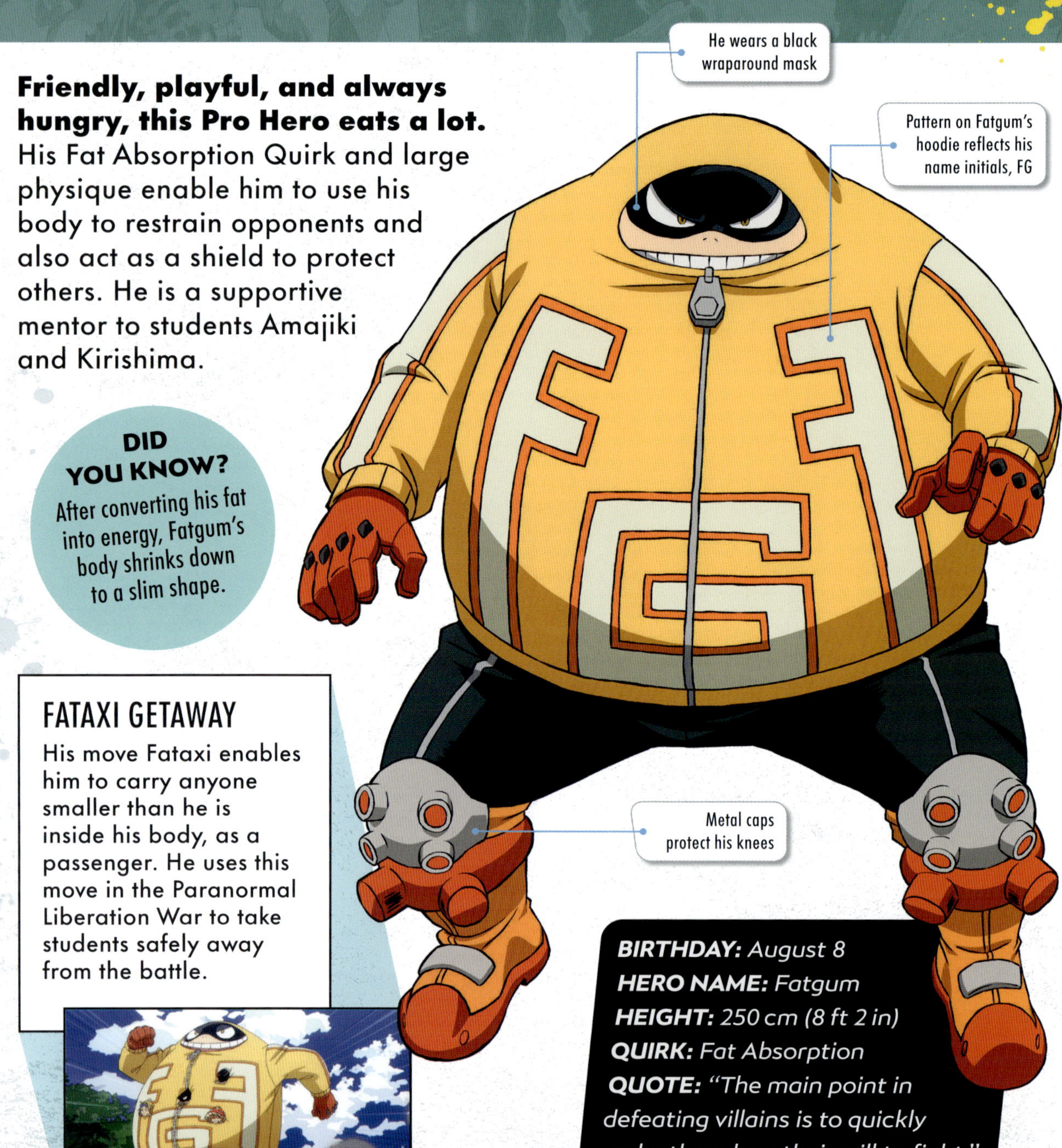

DID YOU KNOW?

After converting his fat into energy, Fatgum's body shrinks down to a slim shape.

FATAXI GETAWAY

His move Fataxi enables him to carry anyone smaller than he is inside his body, as a passenger. He uses this move in the Paranormal Liberation War to take students safely away from the battle.

BIRTHDAY: *August 8*
HERO NAME: *Fatgum*
HEIGHT: *250 cm (8 ft 2 in)*
QUIRK: *Fat Absorption*
QUOTE: *"The main point in defeating villains is to quickly make them lose their will to fight."*

Ryukyu

A Doragoon flying legend

Four claws cover one side of her face and transform into her dragon claw when she activates her Quirk

She has small black wings on either side of her head

Her costume has yellow claw patterns around the neck and on the skirt

When Ryukyu activates her Quirk, her human body transforms into that of a dragon, giving her sharp claws, jaws, and the ability to fly. In her dragon form, Ryukyu is strong and can withstand powerful blows. Despite her magnificence, she is always kind and humble.

BATTLE MODE

Ryukyu transforms into a dragon to battle Katsukame during the Shie Hassaikai raid. She uses her strength to match his power and works with Uraraka and Asui to defeat him.

DID YOU KNOW?

Ryukyu is the second highest-ranking female Pro Hero behind Mirko.

BIRTHDAY: *September 22*
HERO NAME: *Ryukyu*
HEIGHT: *166 cm (5 ft 5 in)*
QUIRK: *Dragon*
QUOTE: *"Team Ryukyu is heeding their call."*

Bubble Girl

Can stop villains with her lethal bubbles

Her Bubble Quirk allows her to create bubbles filled with the aroma of something she has smelled at least once. As one of Sir Nighteye's sidekicks, Bubble Girl works at his hero agency and helps him with his investigations. She remains at Sir Nighteye's agency when Pro Hero Centipeder takes over.

DID YOU KNOW?
She has a cheerful personality but can sometimes lack humor and ends up being punished by Sir Nighteye.

A transparent visor with air holes on either side

The yellow on her shorts matches the edging on her boots

Plain dark-blue gloves

BUBBLE TROUBLE

During the Shie Hassaikai raid, Bubble Girl shows how she can use her combat skills alongside her Quirk to give support to the more powerful Pro Heroes.

BIRTHDAY: *April 23*
HERO NAME: *Bubble Girl*
HEIGHT: *167 cm (5 ft 8 in)*
QUIRK: *Bubble*
QUOTE: *"I will make sure they stay down here."*

Centipeder

His binding ability has villains all wrapped up

Cool, calm, collected Centipeder is a sidekick at Sir Nighteye's agency and eventually goes on to run it. His Centipede Quirk gives him extra-long limbs and his Ultimate Move, Centicoil, enables him to restrain opponents by coiling around them and trapping them tightly.

NIGHTEYE AGENCY

In charge of training Bubble Girl, Centipeder also undertakes investigations in the agency and is central to uncovering Eri's location in the Shie Hassaikai hideout.

BIRTHDAY: *June 4*
HERO NAME: *Centipeder*
HEIGHT: *205 cm (6 ft 9 in)*
QUIRK: *Centipede*
QUOTE: *"Following our stakeout, we know when the guy will be at home."*

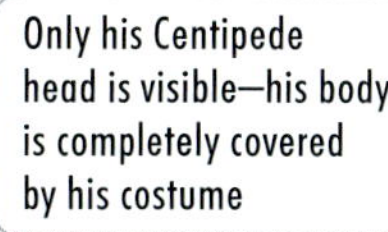

White gloves cover his hands

His hero costume is a smart black tuxedo

DID YOU KNOW?

Thanks to his animalistic Quirk, Centipeder has super-quick reflexes.

Locklock

With one quick touch he can lock everything down

This Pro Hero is a caring dad and is confident in his abilities as a father and Pro Hero. He is proud of his abilities and his Lockdown Quirk, which enables him to lock any nonliving thing in place with just one touch.

HERO RAID

During the Shie Hassaikai Raid, Locklock uses his Deadbolt move to secure a passageway for the Pro Heroes to pass through. But when Himiko Toga launches a surprise attack on him, he is injured and can no longer fight.

He wears locks for earrings

Three keys dangle from his red necklace

His shoulder pads have a lock-shaped emblem on them

Keyhole patterns on his knees

DID YOU KNOW?
His Deadbolt move stops opponents from using the environment against him.

BIRTHDAY: *June 9*
HERO NAME: *Locklock*
HEIGHT: *173 cm (5 ft 8 in)*
QUIRK: *Lockdown*
QUOTE: *"This area won't move again."*

Gang Orca

His ultrasonic waves can stun his enemies

A powerful and intimidating Pro Hero, Gang Orca's Orcinus Quirk gives him the power and abilities of a killer whale. His ultrasonic sound waves can be used like echolocation to find villains and also to stun his opponents during combat. He is No. 12 on the Japanese Hero Billboard Chart.

Hooded cloak has the features of a killer whale

His collar is decorated with diamond shapes that look like teeth

TOUGH TEACHER

Gang Orca's aggressive approach when training students can be intimidating. He sets the students who failed their Provisional Hero License exam the task of winning over some troubled students at Masegaki Elementary School. He is impressed and pleased when they succeed. Underneath his hard exterior, he has a kind heart.

BIRTHDAY: *October 29*
HERO NAME: *Gang Orca*
HEIGHT: *202 cm (6 ft 8 in)*
QUIRK: *Orcinus*
QUOTE: *"Continue to seek excellence."*

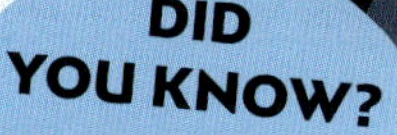

DID YOU KNOW?

Prolonged exposure to dryness can weaken him.

Death Arms

The punching Pro Hero with super strength

DID YOU KNOW?
Jiro finds Death Arms to be a tough trainer when she interns with him.

A muscular Pro Hero, Death Arms' weapon is his super-strong body. His Death Arms Quirk gives him amazing physical strength, enabling him to demolish things with ease. His enhanced strength makes him highly effective in combat and rescue operations, as he can clear debris and break through obstacles to reach and save civilians.

His costume resembles that of a construction worker

Thick wrist cuffs with striped pattern match his belt and bandanna

COMFORTING ARMS

Death Arms consoles Mt. Lady when she's upset at not getting the recognition she feels she deserves at the Japanese Hero Billboard Chart.

BIRTHDAY: *January 11*
HERO NAME: *Death Arms*
HEIGHT: *205 cm (6 ft 9 in)*
QUIRK: *Undecided*
QUOTE: *"A hero must practice and train every day!"*

Backdraft

The dedicated fire-fighting hero

A water cannon is strapped to his back

He wears a red protective hat and his costume is styled like that of a firefighter

DID YOU KNOW?

As well as being a Pro Hero, Backdraft works at the Musatafu Fire Department.

He has taps for hands

His water pumplike Quirk enables him to shoot out water, which he can then manipulate to put out fires. Backdraft's water-based Quirk is essential in managing the aftermath of battles and ensuring public safety.

BIRTHDAY: *March 7*
HERO NAME: *Backdraft*
HEIGHT: *165 cm (5 ft 5 in)*
QUIRK: *Undecided*
QUOTE: *"Let's contain the damage."*

FIRST RESPONDER

When Bakugo is attacked by the Sludge Villain, Backdraft works hard to put out the fire and ensure everyone's safety.

Mandalay

A telepathic hero who can get into your head

Calm and gentle Mandalay is the leader of the Wild Wild Pussycats, a team that specializes in mountain rescues. Her Telepath Quirk enables her to send messages straight into the minds of others, which helps distract and confuse them during battles.

MIND CONTROL

The Wild Wild Pussycats are part of Endeavor's team that raid the Jaku General Hospital. Mandalay is able to communicate with the entire hospital, thanks to her Quirk.

BIRTHDAY: *May 1*
HERO NAME: *Mandalay*
HEIGHT: *168 cm (5 ft 6 in)*
QUIRK: *Telepath*
QUOTE: *"In the name of the Pro Hero Eraser Head you are granted permission to engage in combat."*

DID YOU KNOW?
Mandalay is Kota Izumi's aunt and has taken care of him since he lost his parents.

Her cat-paw gloves can be used to slash enemies

Markings under her eyes resemble whiskers

Her cat's tail pokes out from the back of her mini skirt

Knee- high boots lined with pink fur

Ragdoll

The data specialist with amazing analytical skills

With a mind made for data, Ragdoll is a popular member of the Wild Wild Pussycats. Constantly moving, she is the most energetic member of her team. Her Search Quirk enabled her to monitor the weak points and location of up to 100 people at a time, until All For One stole it.

Ragdoll draws markings on her face to create whiskers

Her gloves are giant cat paws

Her utility belt has useful pouches

STOLEN SKILLS

Before losing her Quirk, Ragdoll excelled in rescue missions as she could use her abilities to search and find victims. Now she supports her team with her admin skills.

DID YOU KNOW

Ragdoll is kidnapped, along with Bakugo, by the Vanguard Action Squad whey they raid their Summer Training Camp.

BIRTHDAY: *April 8*
HERO NAME: *Ragdoll*
HEIGHT: *166 cm (5 ft 5 in)*
QUIRK: *Search*
QUOTE: *"The cat helper is here."*

Pixie-Bob

Her command of the earth leaves villains grounded

With the ability to create huge earth monsters, thanks to her Earthflow Quirk, Pixie-Bob is able to offer ranged support in combat situations. Her wacky and hyperactive personality make her appear eccentric to others.

GROUNDBREAKING

As well as for search and rescue, Pixie-Bob uses her Quirk to control the ground and its movements. Her skills are put to the test when she has to try to stop Tomura Shigaraki's Decay Quirk destroying the Jaku General Hospital.

BIRTHDAY: *June 26*
HERO NAME: *Pixie-Bob*
HEIGHT: *167 cm (5 ft 6 in)*
QUIRK: *Earthflow*
QUOTE: *"Leave it to me! My fur's standing on end."*

DID YOU KNOW?
Sensitive about how long the Wild Wild Pussycats have been a team, Pixie-Bob tells Class 1-A she is still 18 at heart.

Two blue dots on her cheeks

She wears a light-blue version of the Pussycats' team costume

Chunky platform boots

Tiger

The only combat specialist in the Pussycats' team

Tiger is a transgender Pro Hero, and his powerful muscles and flexibility make him a useful ally in combat situations. Tiger's Pilabody Quirk enables him to stretch, bend, and flatten his body in impossible ways. A master of martial arts, his Ultimate Move is called Cat Combat.

DID YOU KNOW?
During the Summer Training Camp, Tiger trains the students with strength-oriented Quirks.

BIRTHDAY: *February 29*
HERO NAME: *Tiger*
HEIGHT: *190 cm (6 ft 3 in)*
QUIRK: *Pilabody*
QUOTE: *"Secretly and unknowingly we arrive."*

TEAMWORK

Tiger fights back when the Vanguard Action Squad attack during the Summer Training Camp. Pixie-Bob is injured, but Tiger and Mandalay eventually defeat Magne and Spinner.

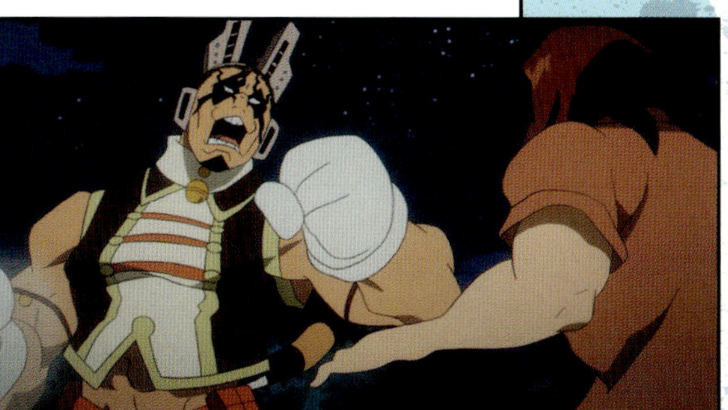

Tiger wears a brown version of the Pussycats' hero costume

His large hands are coverd by cat-paw gloves

Six-pack and rippling muscles are always on display to intimidate opponents

Fourth Kind

Villains can't handle this chivalrous hero

Thanks to his muscular four arms, Fourth Kind packs a mean punch. Impatient and easily angered, Fourth Kind runs his own hero agency. He takes part in the raid of the Gunga Mountain Villa when called up for duty.

He wears a thick gold ring on each of his 16 fingers and 4 thumbs

Three yellow diamond shapes brighten up his dark tie

His hero costume consists of a suit with extra sleeves for his four arms

BIRTHDAY: *February 16*
HERO NAME: *Fourth Kind*
HEIGHT: *184 cm (6 ft)*
QUIRK: *Undecided*
QUOTE: *"Your Quirks are good punching bags."*

TOUGH BOSS

Fourth Kind is tough on Kirishima and Tetsutetsu when they intern at his hero agency. His high standards and professional attitude to his work make him a demanding mentor.

DID YOU KNOW?
He sees community service as an important part of being a hero and helping society.

DID YOU KNOW?
His hero agency specializes in armed combat.

Gunhead

Hero and armed combat specialist

His mask has four holes with protruding gun muzzles

Gunhead's Gatling Quirk gives him the ability to shoot bullets made of keratin out of his arms. Despite his tough and intimidating exterior, Gunhead is extremely friendly and is a supportive mentor to the students at U.A. High School.

He wears a body vest with padded armor

BIRTHDAY: *May 7*
HERO NAME: *Gunhead*
HEIGHT: *191 cm (6 ft 3 in)*
QUIRK: *Gatling*
QUOTE: *"The most important thing is physical strength."*

STRONG MENTOR

Gunhead instructs Uraraka in hand-to-hand combat skills so she can overpower opponents quickly and defend herself.

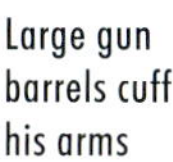

Large gun barrels cuff his arms

Uwabami

The Pro Hero who is also a media star

Uwabami has a trio of snakes living on her head. The snakes' amazing animal senses enable Uwabami to locate disaster victims and criminals quickly. She often prioritizes her media jobs over her Pro Hero work and confesses to choosing Yaoyorozu and Kendo as her interns because they look cute.

DID YOU KNOW?
Uwabami appears in a TV commercial with Yaoyorozu and Kendo.

BIRTHDAY: *December 9*
HERO NAME: *Uwabami*
HEIGHT: *170 cm (5 ft 7 in)*
QUIRK: *Undecided*
QUOTE: *"There are two down here. Over there too!"*

SERPENT RESCUE

Her Quirk is invaluable in locating victims trapped in the debris caused by the fight between All For One and All Might in Kamino.

Manual

This steady Pro Hero can handle anything

Manual's waterlike Quirk enables him to manipulate water and helps him to keep flames under control. He has his own Hero Agency in Hosu and offers Iida an internship. He is surprised when he accepts it, but then realizes Iida has come to Hosu only so he can catch Stain.

TEAM EFFORT

Manual uses his Quirk to help stop Eraser Head's eyes from drying out when he is locating Tomura Shigaraki during the Paranormal Liberation War.

DID YOU KNOW?

Manual worries about Iida and warns him about seeking vengeance with Stain.

BIRTHDAY: *December 5*
HERO NAME: *Manual*
HEIGHT: *176 cm (5 ft 9 in)*
QUIRK: *Undecided*
QUOTE: *"That is why, no matter what reason, heroes must not use their Quirks for themselves."*

TEACHERS

Present Mic
Snipe
Cementos
Many of the Pro Heroes work as teachers at U.A. High School. They challenge and inspire their students as they train to become Pro Heroes.

All Might

The legendary hero and the Symbol of Peace

Two distinct hair bangs stick up from his head, like horns

His costume's colors are red, white, and blue

Yellow boots match his arm wings and belt

All Might inherited his One For All Quirk, which gives him his impressive power and strength. When he recognizes true heroism in Midoriya, he passes his Quirk on to him then dedicates himself to training his prodigy and the students at U.A. High School.

BIRTHDAY: *June 10*
HERO NAME: *All Might*
HEIGHT: *220 cm (7 ft 3 in)*
QUIRK: *One For All*
QUOTE: *"I am here."*

DEADLY ENEMIES

After his first battle with All For One, All Might suffered terrible injuries. Six years later, All Might confronts him again in Kamino, determined to put him behind bars. All For One taunts All Might for his diminished state, but All Might doesn't give up and finally defeats him.

DID YOU KNOW?
When he was a student, All Might was trained by Gran Torino.

All Might's hair bangs flop down when he is in his True Form

SYMBOL OF PEACE

All Might is determined to put an end to violence in the world. He thinks if he saves people with a smile and shows no fear he will inspire everyone to have hope and to live together in harmony.

DID YOU KNOW?

All Might is the eighth holder of the One For All Quirk, which was passed on to him by his mentor, Nana Shimura.

Trousers hang loosely off his body due to his weight loss

All Might is worried about Midoriya when he goes after All For One alone. He tries his best to support him, bringing Midoriya food when he can, to help keep his strength up. He cannot make him rest, though, and feels helpless.

Eraser Head

He can erase Quirks with just one look

This Pro Hero's Erasure Quirk enables him to block his opponent from activating their Quirk. Eraser Head then quickly takes them down with his binding cloth. Class 1-A's calm and caring teacher is as smart in the classroom as he is in battle and pushes his students to get the best out of them.

DID YOU KNOW?
He uses his goggles in battle so enemies don't know who he is looking at.

When he's not wearing his yellow goggles, he hangs them around his neck

His binding cloth is always wrapped around his neck, ready for action

BIRTHDAY: *November 8*
HERO NAME: *Eraser Head*
HEIGHT: *183 cm (6 ft)*
QUIRK: *Erasure*
QUOTE: *"It was a logical lie to make you fully use your Quirks."*

HERO COURSE

Eraser Head tells his students that U.A. High School is known for its unrestricted style and training.

Present Mic

A booming voice that can destroy eardrums

Present Mic's voice is his weapon. His Voice Quirk enables him to make sounds that explode his opponent's hearing and cause damage miles away. Present Mic never switches off and often poses as he chatters away, keeping up his radio persona at all times. Excitable and energetic, he can always be counted on to hype up the crowd.

Cool orange shades and protective headphones

EXPLOSIVE VOICE

Present Mic tries to stop the Nomu attack in the Jaku General Hospital. He uses his DJ Punch and Loud Voice moves to break up the lab of Kyudai Garaki, All For One's doctor.

Speaker is used to direct his speech when using his Quirk

BIRTHDAY: *July 7*
HERO NAME: *Present Mic*
HEIGHT: *185 cm (6 ft 1 in)*
QUIRK: *Voice*
QUOTE: *"Hey! Get ready, audience!"*

DID YOU KNOW?
Present Mic is always in charge of commentary for school events.

Midnight

Puts enemies to sleep with her bewitching Quirk

Midnight's handcuffs double up as bracelets

Midnight takes her teaching and Pro Hero roles seriously. She uses her charm and Somnambulist Quirk to defeat her opponents. With just a single breath, she activates her Quirk and can quickly spread her sleep-inducing aroma, which effectively knocks out enemies without the need for combat.

She uses her hand fans to spread her sleep-inducing aroma

Gold-studded utility belt

BIRTHDAY: *March 9*
HERO NAME: *Midnight*
HEIGHT: *175 cm (5 ft 9 in)*
QUIRK: *Somnambulist*
QUOTE: *"Just one breath will be the end of you."*

DID YOU KNOW?
Midnight helps the students of Class 1-A choose their hero names.

GROUP MISSION

Midnight is part of the team of Pro Heroes charged with attacking the Gunga Mountain Villa—the headquarters of the Paranormal Liberation Front.

Cementos

A rock-hard, stony exterior but a heart of gold

This block-headed hero can control concrete. His Cement Quirk enables him to touch concrete and instantly change its hardness so he can manipulate it to form anything he wants. His quick reflexes also mean he's able to block attacks, protecting himself and others.

DID YOU KNOW?
As well as being a Pro Hero, Cementos teaches at U.A. High School and was a judge at the Entrance Exams.

BIRTHDAY: *March 22*
HERO NAME: *Cementos*
HEIGHT: *185 cm (6 ft 1 in)*
QUIRK: *Cement*
QUOTE: *"I'll stop any scum moves."*

SOLID DEFENSE

Cementos manages to trap the villain Geten in a huge block of his cement during the Paranormal Liberation War. He is then struck and flattened by ice.

Snipe

A gun-toting hero who shoots to hit

DID YOU KNOW?
Snipe can lock onto a target up to 600 m (1,969 ft) away.

Level-headed and experienced, Snipe is in charge of the third-year students at U.A. High School. A Pro Hero with cowboy-like tendencies, his Homing Quirk allows him to lock onto any target he can see and make any projectile he releases hit the target.

ON TARGET

Snipe's Quirk makes him a supportive combat ally, but he is also a protective force for the students. He is responsible for ensuring the U.A. High School Festival runs smoothly and the students remain safe.

BIRTHDAY: *November 7*
HERO NAME: *Snipe*
HEIGHT: *182 cm (6 ft)*
QUIRK: *Homing*
QUOTE: *"There are many people who don't know what to do with their Quirks."*

Ectoplasm

The math teacher who can clone an army

Ectoplasm is a brave and loyal Pro Hero, always eager to teach others. His amazing Clone Quirk enables him to spew ectoplasm from his mouth and transform it into clones of himself. His clones act as extensions of his body and operate in a similar way to a hive mind.

TOP TEACHER

Ectoplasm creates clones for the students to battle to help them train for the Provisional Hero License Exam. He tells his students they need to develop super moves and techniques if they want to succeed in combat.

His mask covers his entire head and matches his bodysuit under his cloak

DID YOU KNOW?
Ectoplasm can make up to 36 clones of himself in one go, or one giant clone in his Giant Bite Detention move.

BIRTHDAY: *March 23*
HERO NAME: *Ectoplasm*
HEIGHT: *180 cm (5 ft 11 in)*
QUIRK: *Clones*
QUOTE: *"Prepare your determination and resolve."*

Vlad King

The homeroom teacher of Class 1-B

With his Blood Control Quirk Vlad King can weaponize his own blood, taking down enemies and influencing the movement of villains as easily as he influences his class students. Vlad King is proud and passionate about his strength, abilities, and dual roles as a Pro Hero and teacher in society.

RIVAL CLASSES

Vlad King is in a constant competition to beat his friend and colleague Eraser Head's Class 1-A. Both teachers share a determined and passionate commitment to their students.

BIRTHDAY: *November 10*
HERO NAME: *Vlad King*
HEIGHT: *194 cm (6 ft 4 in)*
QUIRK: *Blood Control*
QUOTE: *"Will my students' furious attacks finally crush Class A?!"*

His hero costume exposes his strong chest muscles

Three-piece metal belt

DID YOU KNOW?
Vlad King's blood loss does not weaken him.

Recovery Girl

Serious injuries are no match for her healing skills

DID YOU KNOW?
As well as her Quirk abilities, Recovery Girl knows how to perform medical procedures.

Recovery Girl is the legendary U.A. High School nurse. Her Heal Quirk is constantly in demand with so many students sustaining injuries during battles and training. With just one kiss, she can speed up the body's natural healing process, enabling her to heal broken limbs and deep wounds.

BIRTHDAY: *April 4*
HERO NAME: *Recovery Girl*
HEIGHT: *115 cm (3 ft 9 in)*
QUIRK: *Heal*
QUOTE: *"Because of the special circumstances, I can't get mad."*

Wide purple shades

She uses a syringe as a walking stick

HEALING SMOOCH

Recovery Girl heals Todoroki with a lip-smacking smooch after he is injured during Joint Combat Training between Class 1-A and 1-B. She always offers a protein bar to her patients, too, to help with their recovery.

Thirteen

The space hero who rescues civilians in disasters

Thirteen's Black Hole Quirk means she can suck anything down to atomic level. When Kurogiri attacks at the Unforeseen Simulation Joint, Thirteen assists in trying to capture Tomura Shigaraki and Kurogiri to get the Class 1-A students away from them and danger.

DID YOU KNOW?
Thirteen developed her own training facility—The Unforeseen Simulation Joint.

RESCUE HERO

When Midoriya returns to U.A. High School after searching for All For One, Thirteen is the first teacher who welcomes him and explains that the school is now using U.A. Emergency Security System for evacuees.

BIRTHDAY: *February 3*
HERO NAME: *Thirteen*
QUIRK: *Black Hole*
HEIGHT: *180 cm (5 ft 11 in)*
QUOTE: *"We'll learn to use your Quirks to rescue people."*

Nezu

The small but mighty Principal of U.A. High School

Nezu is the only animal to manifest a Quirk. He always shows great humanity and kindness when dealing with his students and is very protective of them. He builds the U.A. Barrier, which will trigger large walls to rise up and seal off the entrance should anyone try to enter the school without a student ID or visitor pass.

BIRTHDAY: *January 1*
QUIRK: *High Specs*
HEIGHT: *85 cm (2 ft 9 in)*
QUOTE: *"Either something wicked came in or they're declaring war."*

He has a scar on his right eye

Nezu dresses in a formal suit, white shirt, and tie

Six gold buttons fasten his waistcoat

DID YOU KNOW?
Nezu paid for all the design and construction fees for the U.A. Barrier.

NATURAL BORN LEADER

Nezu built the U.A. Barrier to prevent the League of Villains from getting into the school. It can also operate as a shelter for evacuees.

Hound Dog

The Pro Hero with a rapid response rate

A skilled youth counselor at U.A. High School, Hound Dog offers support and guidance to his students. But when he gets angry, he can lose the ability to speak and communicates instead with doglike barks and growls, which can leave the students feeling terrified rather than reassured.

Hound Dog wears a muzzle over his nose and mouth

A fur gilet covers his upper body and matches the fur on his boots

DID YOU KNOW?
His animal mutation gives him the super senses of a dog.

A NOSE FOR TROUBLE

Responsible for the security at the U.A. High School Festival, Hound Dog is quick to sniff out intruders. He investigates with Ectoplasm and discovers criminals Gentle Criminal and La Brava lurking.

Two-tone fingerless gloves

Brown, knee-high, fur-lined boots

BIRTHDAY: *November 15*
HERO NAME: *Hound Dog*
HEIGHT: *196 cm (6 ft 5 in)*
QUIRK: *Dog*
QUOTE: *"It's the teacher's duty to protect their students."*

Power Loader

The engineering expert and inventor

DID YOU KNOW?
Power Loader oversees the Support department at U.A. High School.

Talented and creative, Power Loader's Iron Claw Quirk enables him to transform his fingertips into huge, powerful claws, making him efficient in digging and construction. He utilizes his skills in his role at U.A. High School, where he designs and maintains costumes and support items for the students and Pro Heroes.

BIRTHDAY: *September 17*
HERO NAME: *Power Loader*
HEIGHT: *155 cm (5 ft 1 in)*
QUIRK: *Iron Claw*
QUOTE: *"Innovators are not bound by existing ideas."*

DESIGN SUPPORT

Power Loader is a supportive mentor to Hatsume. He is always there to help her with her technical needs as well as those of his students at key points in their training, like during the Provisional Hero License Exam.

VILLAINS

Dabi
Twice
All For One
Deadly and dangerous, these antiheroes unite, determined to bring chaos to the world and destroy hero society.

Tomura Shigaraki

The villainous leader who turns everything to dust

With just one touch, Tomura Shigaraki can use his Decay Quirk to obliterate anyone or anything. His goal is simple: to destroy society. Groomed by All For One from a young age to be his successor, Tomura Shigaraki is determined to create his own future and not be controlled by anyone.

His dead father's hand creates a mask for his face

BRUTE FORCE

Following All For One's capture, Tomura Shigaraki takes over as leader of the League of Villains. When he discovers that All For One has left him the wild Gigantomachia, he initially thinks he's more trouble than he's worth.

His costume is made up of the hands of all the victims he has killed, including those of his own family

BIRTHDAY: *April 4*
AFFILIATION: *League of Villains*
HEIGHT: *175 cm (5 ft 9 in)*
QUIRK: *Decay*
QUOTE: *"Destroy everything!"*

ENEMY ENCOUNTER

Midoriya unleashes his Blackwhip move to defend himself against Tomura Shigaraki, who is determined to steal Midoriya's One For All Quirk for himself.

His hair changes from blue to white

He picks off his enemies one by one, until he is left as the true antihero leader. While Tomura Shigaraki strives to destroy, Midoriya is his mirror opposite and only wants to help others. Both inherit their mentor's Quirks. Tomura Shigaraki is intent on destroying Midoriya, but the hero in training wants to end Tomura Shigaraki's suffering.

Long, red coat with a fur-lined collar

DID YOU KNOW?

Tomura Shigaraki was unable to control his Quirk as a young boy, which led to the death of his entire family.

Dabi

A pyromaniac villain intent on revenge

Inspired by Stain's beliefs and impressed by Tomura Shigaraki when he defeats the Meta Liberation Army, Dabi fights alongside his villainous allies to destroy the hero society. He uses his Flashfire Fist move to generate deadly flame attacks when in combat and is capable of generating huge firewalls.

Purple burn scars on his face, neck, and chest caused by his inability to control his Quirk when young

DOUBLE-CROSSED

Hawks uses Dabi to infiltrate the League of Villains as a double agent. Dabi is furious when Hawks kills Twice and he discovers the truth.

A long, dark, tattered cloak, pants, and boots

BIRTHDAY: *January 18*
HEIGHT: *176 cm (5 ft 9 in)*
QUIRK: *Blueflame*
AFFILIATION: *League of Villains*
QUOTE: *"We'll let them know that their peace lies in the palm of our hands."*

DID YOU KNOW?

Like Stain, Dabi believes that anyone who is motivated by self-interest cannot be a hero.

THE UGLY TRUTH

Dabi broadcasts the truth about his childhood and taunts Endeavor that everyone will know about his ruthless ambition and the pain he has caused his family.

When Dabi reveals himself as Endeavor's eldest son Toya, his hair changes to gray

Large metal cuffs around his biceps

Broken by the abandonment of his father, Endeavor, as a child Dabi tried to master his Quirk but succeeded only in hurting himself both physically and mentally. His quest to live up to his father's demanding expectations caused years of suffering. His Blueflame Quirk is powerful, but if he overuses it, he can get burned.

During the Paranormal Liberation War, his costume was updated with stitches

Himiko Toga

The young girl who will ingest your blood

A toothy neck brace is attached to canisters and needles that assist with her Quirk

Toga expresses her love and admiration in an unusual way, by ingesting someone's blood to turn into them. Her shape-shifting Transform Quirk makes her a master of disguise and stealth, and a dangerous opponent. When she presents herself to Tomura Shigaraki and the villains, she tells them she finds life difficult and wants to make the world an easier place to live. She wants to become like those she loves, even if it means hurting them.

A green box of knives strapped to her thigh

DID YOU KNOW?
When she transforms, Toga can also copy the voices of her victims.

QUIRK AWAKENING

When Toga's Quirk undergoes an awakening, not only can she transform into others but also take on their Quirk abilities. She uses a vial of Uraraka's blood and her Zero Gravity Quirk to take on Curious and the Meta Liberation Army.

BIRTHDAY: *August 7*
HEIGHT: *157 cm (5 ft 2 in)*
QUIRK: *Transform*
AFFILIATION: *League of Villains*
QUOTE: *"I want this world to be an easier place to live."*

Twice

A dangerous villain who is double the trouble

Twice wears a mask to make him feel whole

Black bodysuit with gray trim

His measuring tapes are stored in his wristbands

Twice's Double Quirk enables him to make an exact copy of anything, so long as he knows its measurements and characteristics. After a life of petty solo crime, Twice joined the League of Villains as they valued his abilities and accepted him for who he was.

SAD MAN'S PARADE

Twice's Quirk enables him to double lots of things. He can clone himself fastest, though, as he knows himself best. He uses his Ultimate Move, Sad Man's Parade, to create a clone army of himself to help Shigaraki defeat the Meta Liberation Army.

DID YOU KNOW?

Without his mask, Twice's split personalities argue with each other, so he needs to keep his head wrapped up.

BIRTHDAY: *May 10*
HEIGHT: *178 cm (5 ft 10 in)*
QUIRK: *Double*
AFFILIATION: *League of Villains*
QUOTE: *"If I don't wrap myself up, I'll split into two."*

Spinner

A fierce fighter with a lizardlike Quirk

DID YOU KNOW?
Spinner believes if he hadn't joined the League of Villains, he would be a nobody.

Weapon-wielding Spinner looks like a gecko, and his Quirk enables him to climb and stick to walls. A follower rather than a leader, he often feels insecure about his skills and looks to others for motivation. He is a big fan of Stain, and it is his ideology that inspires him to join the League of Villains. He questions whether the villains' beliefs are aligned to Stain's, though, when they attack the police during their capture of Overhaul after the Shie Hassaikai raid.

He wears a red scarf and bandages to look like his hero Stain

The sword on his back is made from many smaller blades

Large pads protect his knees

DEVOTED FOLLOWER

Following the Tarturus prison break, Spinner loyally protects Tomura Shigaraki while he recovers after All For One has taken control of his body.

BIRTHDAY: *August 8*
HEIGHT: *174 cm (5 ft 9 in)*
QUIRK: *Gecko*
AFFILIATION: *League of Villains*
QUOTE: *"I'm Spinner. The one who'll make his dream come true."*

Mr. Compress

The engaging entertainer who likes to surprise

Mr. Compress was a talented thief before joining The League of Villains. His Compress Quirk gives him the ability to compress an area or person into a marble. He is part of the Vanguard Action Squad, an elite group of villains who attack the U.A. High School students during their Summer Training. He kidnaps Bakugo and Tokoyami, wanting to show them there is an alternative way of thinking to that of the hero society.

SPEEDY SHOWMAN

A master of surprise, he catches many Pro Heroes off their guard. He successfully frees his villain allies from Best Jeanist's binds before he's finally taken down by Big 3 student Togata during the Paranormal Liberation War.

BIRTHDAY: *October 8*
HEIGHT: *181 cm (5 ft 11 in)*
QUIRK: *Compress*
AFFILIATION: *League of Villains*
QUOTE: *"It's time for Mr. Compress's once-in-a-lifetime escape act."*

DID YOU KNOW?
Mr. Compress loses his arm to Overhaul when the League of Villains approach the Shie Hassaikai leader to join with them.

All For One

Pure evil and the ruler of the underworld

All For One's face is mostly scar tissue, which he covers up with a mask

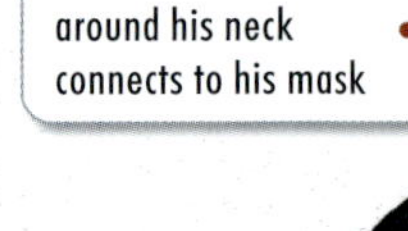

By stealing the Quirks of others, All For One manipulates villains to do his bidding. He wields a sinister power over his huge network, which he likes to control from the shadows. All For One can combine multiple Quirks to use effectively together in combat, while using his Warp Quirk enables him to create portals with a black liquid, which can transport his loyal followers. He is constantly plotting the downfall of All Might and the hero society.

MASTER THIEF

All For One can redistribute his stolen Quirks. Midoriya experiences a flashback to when All For One bestowed stolen Quirks on his brother Yoichi.

DID YOU KNOW?

He rescued Tomura Shigaraki from the streets after he became an orphan and gave him his family's hands.

BIRTHDAY: *Unknown*
HEIGHT: *Unknown*
AFFILIATION: *League of Villains*
QUIRK: *All For One*
QUOTE: *"You are the one who will cause this world to grieve."*

He wears black shoes and a sleek, dark suit

Gigantomachia

A rampaging, unstoppable giant of destruction

Jagged, rough, rocklike muscles

DID YOU KNOW?
All For One hid Gigantomachia away, planning for when he could return and serve Tomura Shigaraki.

As All For One's loyal bodyguard, Gigantomachia mows down anyone in his, or his master's, way. Strong and resilient, he is able to withstand holding multiple Quirks at once and uses them to great effect to defeat his enemies. His Endurance Quirk gives him lots of energy and increased stamina, while his Dog Quirk gives him heightened senses. At first, he won't fight alongside Tomura Shigaraki, refusing to accept him as a worthy successor to All For One.

Simple black pants show off his muscular strength

Large, pawlike bare feet

VILLAIN ALLEGIANCE

After witnessing Tomura Shigaraki's destruction of Deika City and his battle with Re-Destro, Gigantomachia finally accepts Tomura Shigaraki has what it takes to follow in All For One's footsteps.

BIRTHDAY: *Unknown*
HEIGHT: *Unknown*
QUIRK: *Endurance and more*
AFFILIATION: *League of Villains*
QUOTE: *"I've searched so long, now I've found you at last."*

Kurogiri

The Nomu villain who can bend space and transport others

Created by All For One to watch over Tomura Shigaraki, Kurogiri is intensely loyal to them both and programmed to take orders only from a select few. His Warp Gate Quirk gives him the ability to create a dark fog from his hands and head, which acts like a portal to transport others to a location of his choosing.

DID YOU KNOW?

Kurogiri 's Quirk is coordinate-based, so he needs to know the exact location of where he opens up a portal.

A tall metal collar rests on his shoulders

He wears a smart shirt, tie, vest, and pants

His body is entirely made from a purple-and-black mist

DEFENDER OF VILLAINS

Kurogiri was created from the dead body of Oboro Shirakumo, a student at U.A. High School. When Gran Torino captures Kurogiri, he asks Eraser Head and Present Mic to question him. He hopes their childhood connection with Oboro Shirakumo will mean they can get Kurogiri to switch allegiances and give them information about the villains.

BIRTHDAY: *Unknown*
HEIGHT: *Unknown*
QUIRK: *Warp Gate*
AFFILIATION: *League of Villains*
QUOTE: *"It's my duty to look after him."*

Stain

The killer who thinks heroes are frauds

DID YOU KNOW?
After the Tartarus prison break, Stain gives All Might information that he discovered in Tartarus about All For One.

Motivated by his desire to rid the world of all heroes, Stain goes on a killing spree to change society. Stain's Bloodcurdle Quirk enables him to paralyze his victims by tasting their blood. The amount of time they remain paralyzed depends on their blood type.

HERO WORSHIP

Stain believes All Might is the only worthy hero and admires him for his desire to help others. He is shocked when he finally meets All Might in his diminished form.

BIRTHDAY: *June 14*
HEIGHT: *182 cm (5 ft 12 in)*
QUIRK: *Bloodcurdle*
AFFILIATION: *League of Villains*
QUOTE: *"What's the meaning of killing without a strong conviction?"*

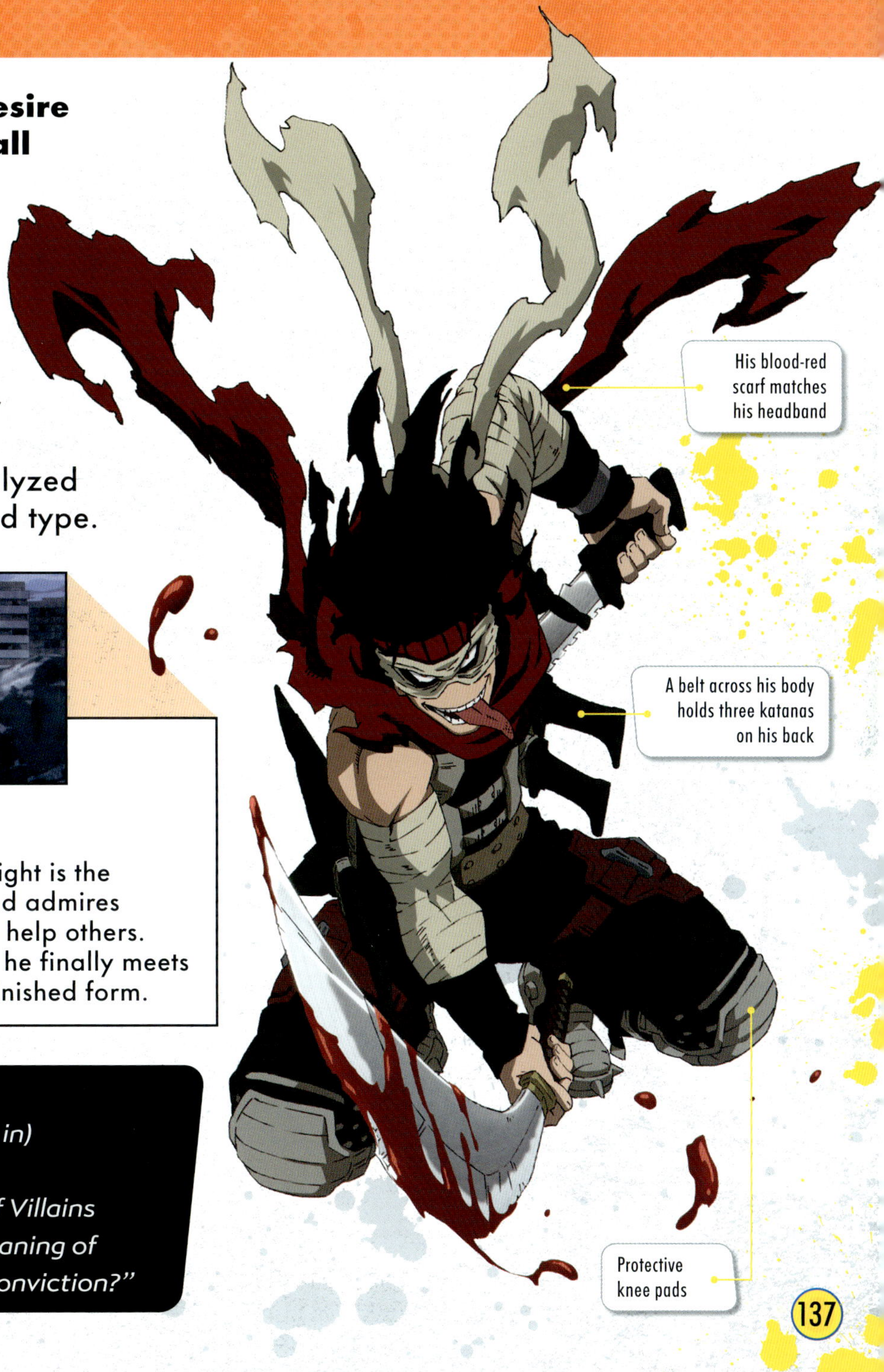

His blood-red scarf matches his headband

A belt across his body holds three katanas on his back

Protective knee pads

Muscular

A pumped-up criminal who loves blood and violence

Muscular's Muscle Augmentation Quirk enables him to amplify and manipulate his muscle layers so they literally pop out of his skin. This gives this brutal villain supreme strength and speed, and enhanced durability. One of the cruelest villains, Muscular enjoys tormenting his opponents before inflicting maximum damage.

DID YOU KNOW?
Muscular lost his left eye when battling Water Hose, Kota's parents, whom he then killed.

He keeps the replacement eye in his pocket

BIRTHDAY: *Unknown*
HEIGHT: *Unknown*
QUIRK: *Muscle Augmentation*
AFFILIATION: *Vanguard Action Squad*
QUOTE: *"I'll torment you for good."*

Muscular wears his jacket tied around his waist to reveal his ripped torso

COLD-BLOODED DESTROYER

After escaping from the prison Tartarus, Muscular is excited to run into Midoriya again—but proves no match for his One For All Quirk and is soon defeated and returned to prison.

Mustard

The toxic villain who proudly poisons the air

DID YOU KNOW?
Mustard isn't immune to his gas and has to wear a mask for protection.

Two oxygen tanks are strapped to his back

Mustard's face is completely hidden by the gas mask he wears as part of his costume

His costume is styled like a school uniform, and comprises a jacket and pants

Mustard's Gas Quirk enables him to quickly spread poison gas in an area to slow down opponents or send them to sleep. Mustard forms part of the Vanguard Action Squad, the group of villains tasked with the mission to attack U.A. High School students and kidnap Bakugo.

BIRTHDAY: *Unknown*
HEIGHT: *Unknown*
QUIRK: *Gas*
AFFILIATION: *Vanguard Action Squad*
QUOTE: *"No matter how great your Quirk is... you're still human."*

DEADLY PRIDE

During the Vanguard Action Squad attack, Mustard is pleased with his abilities and scornful of Tetsutetsu and Kendo when they try to fight back. But when the two students join forces, they finally defeat him.

Overhaul

A reformer who wants to destroy and rebuild

The young leader of the organized crime gang Shie Hassaikai, Overhaul is obsessed with ridding the world of Quirks, believing them to be a curse. He is able to disassemble and reassemble matter so can both destroy and heal. Overhaul is made guardian of Eri, the granddaughter of the former boss of his gang. He pretends to be her father in public but uses her cruelly by extracting her blood to create Quirk-destroying bullets.

His mouth is covered by an embroidered plague face mask to protect him from germs in the air

He wears white surgical gloves to protect his hands from germs too

Casual, plain black pants

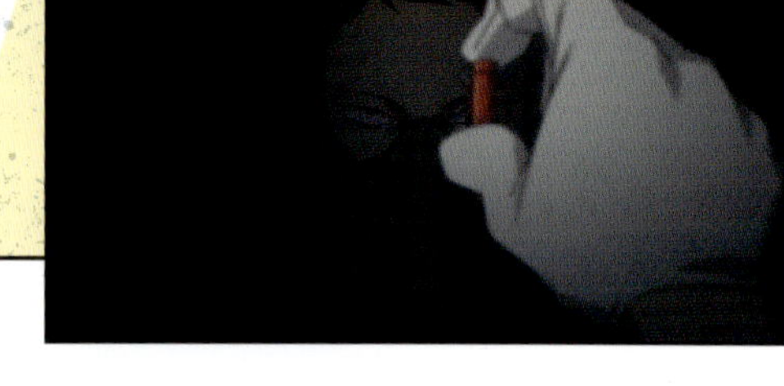

SECRET WEAPON

Overhaul works with Chronostasis to develop bullets that can cancel Quirks forever. He hopes that he can sell them, make a huge profit, and restore his gang to its former glory days.

BIRTHDAY: *March 20*
HEIGHT: *179 cm (5 ft 11 in)*
QUIRK: *Overhaul*
AFFILIATION: *Shie Hassaikai*
QUOTE: *"A goal without a plan is merely a delusion."*

ERI'S CAPTOR

Togato fights Overhaul to protect Eri and take her into his custody. Eri is worried Togata will be killed but is surprised by his strength and the lengths he will go to save her during the Shie Hassaikai raid.

DID YOU KNOW?

Overhaul puts his boss into a coma when he disagrees with his plans for Eri.

Midoriya goes after Overhaul when he tries to escape with Eri during the Shie Hassaikai raid. Eri leaps into Midoriya's arms, and even though Overhaul warns him Eri's Quirk will cause him to disappear, Midoriya refuses to let her go. He battles fiercely with Overhaul, who has taken on a monstrous form. Attacking him with powerful punches, Midoriya is helped and protected by Eri's power and eventually defeats Overhaul and saves Eri.

OVERPOWERED

Tomura Shigaraki and the League of Villains finally seek their revenge on Overhaul. They take his arms and his Quirk-destroying bullets and leave him to be captured by the police, who throw him into the high-security prison Tartarus.

Chronostasis

The time-warping assistant to Overhaul

His Chronostasis Quirk enables the cold-hearted Chronostasis to attack by slowing down the movements of anything he touches with the strands of his hair. He is one of the Eight Bullets, a small gang within the main Shie Hassaikai. He assists Overhaul in his experiments on Eri and is eventually locked up in prison.

DID YOU KNOW?
Stabbing his victims causes them to slow down or freeze.

LOYAL ASSISTANT

When Overhaul visits the League of Villains, Chronostasis jumps in to fight alongside his boss and fellow gang member, Rikiya Katsukame, and shoots Mr. Compress.

BIRTHDAY: *Unknown*
HEIGHT: *Unknown*
QUIRK: *Chronostasis*
AFFILIATION: *Shie Hassaikai*
QUOTE: *"I thought a hero's cape was just them trying to look cool."*

Mimic

A gang member with controlling powers

A loyal and useful member of Overhaul's inner circle in the Shie Hassaikai, Mimic's Quirk allows him to merge his body with objects and control them as if they were extensions of his own body. He also takes a drug that enhances his Quirk, to enable him to take control of larger spaces and structures.

A plague mask is sewn over his face

A black all-in-one covers Mimic's small body

BIRTHDAY: *Unknown*
HEIGHT: *Unknown*
QUIRK: *Mimicry*
AFFILIATION: *Shie Hassaikai*
QUOTE: *"Don't underestimate us."*

NEW RECRUITS

Mimic is distrustful of Himiko Toga and Twice, and unimpressed with their attitudes when they are recruited to the Shie Hassaikai. He demands they explain their Quirks so Overhaul can figure out how best to use them.

DID YOU KNOW?

Mimic takes a trigger drug to enhance his Quirk and his abilities when the Pro Heroes invade the Shie Hassaikai compound.

Rikiya Katsukame

The Shie Hassaikai member who absorbs energy

Recruited by Overhaul into Shie Hassaikai, Katsukame is a loyal gang member with a useful Quirk. His Energy Suction abilities mean he can drain away other people's stamina and strength and use them to increase his own.

BIRTHDAY: *Unknown*
HEIGHT: *Unknown*
QUIRK: *Energy Suction*
AFFILIATION: *Shie Hassaikai*
QUOTE: *"I feel full of energy."*

DID YOU KNOW?
During the Shie Hassaikai raid, he uses a trigger drug that enables him to absorb the energy of Uraraka and Asui without touching them.

Metal shoulder harness

Black tank top

POWERING UP

During the Shie Hassaikai raid, Katsukame absorbs energy from the police force, Uraraka, and Asui before going into battle with Ryukyu and Hado.

Toya Setsuno

There is no limit to what this gang member would steal

Setsuno's Quirk usefully enables him to take something from another's hands and into his possession. This master thief is one of the Eight Bullets of the Shie Hassaikai and works well with its other members. When the Pro Heroes invade Shie Hassaikai's HQ, he fights alongside Hojo and Tabe to battle Amajiki. Setsuno stops Amajiki from defending himself by stealing his clamshell with his Quirk.

DID YOU KNOW?
Setsuno can steal an item only if he can see it and it's not too large.

WRAPPED UP

When Setsuno tries to use his Larceny Quirk to steal police officers' guns during the Shie Hassaikai raid, his Quirk is erased by Eraser Head. After his difficult battle with Amajiki, he ends up being captured and arrested.

BIRTHDAY: *Unknown*
HEIGHT: *Unknown*
QUIRK: *Larceny*
AFFILIATION: *Shie Hassaikai*
QUOTE: *"I'll have you all killed."*

Yu Hojo

The gang member with the rock-hard Quirk

Hojo's Crystallize Quirk enables him to grow hard, sharp crystals on his skin, which he can use to attack and defend. He has an excellent handle on his Quirk and can manipulate his crystals into swords on his arms to use as weapons.

SMOOTH COLLABORATION

When Amajiki takes on three gang members at once during the Shie Hassaikai raid, Hojo works well with Setsuno to catch him off guard. Eventually Amajiki uses Hojo's Quirk against him by eating one of his crystals to create protective armor.

***BIRTHDAY:** Unknown*
***HEIGHT:** Unknown*
***QUIRK:** Crystallize*
***AFFILIATION:** Shie Hassaikai*
***QUOTE:** "Even trash has its pride."*

Soramitsu Tabe

A hungry gang member with a big appetite

Tabe's Food Quirk ensures he can munch his way through any attack. Handy in battle, this Eight Bullets member of the notorious Shie Hassaikai works well with its other members and is fiercely loyal to Overhaul. Like the other gang members, Tabe felt like an outcast before joining the gang and is happy to finally have found somewhere he feels he belongs.

DID YOU KNOW?
Tabe has an iron stomach that can digest anything he munches on.

BIRTHDAY: *Unknown*
HEIGHT: *Unknown*
QUIRK: *Food*
AFFILIATION: *Shie Hassaikai*
QUOTE: *"Octopus, yum."*

BIG BITE

It's not just food that Tabe can gobble down; his huge jaw can bite into anything and consume it quickly. But when Amajiki attacks with his tentacles during the Shie Hassaikai raid, Tabe bites off more than he can chew and is poisoned by the hero in training.

Kendo Rappa

A hot-blooded fighter who loves violence

Unlike Overhaul's other gang members, Rappa is the only member of the Eight Bullets and Shie Hassaikai who has an ulterior motive for joining the gang. He wants to defeat Overhaul and exact his revenge for when Overhaul beat him in a fight when he recruited him for his gang. Rappa keeps challenging Overhaul but has yet to beat him.

Plague mask

Metal gloves cover his hands

STREET FIGHTER

Rappa comes up against Kirishima and Fatgum during the Shie Hassaikai raid. His Strongarm Quirk allows him to land multiple punches at super speeds. Despite sustaining injuries, Rappa looks forward to the time they can fight again.

DID YOU KNOW?
Rappa used to compete in an underground fight club before joining the gang.

BIRTHDAY: *Unknown*
HEIGHT: *Unknown*
QUIRK: *Strongarm*
AFFILIATION: *Shie Hassaikai*
QUOTE: *"I want a fight, a good fight."*

Hekiji Tengai

The defense specialist who keeps his cool

Tengai was assigned by Overhaul to Rappa as a fighting partner. His calm personality balances out Rappa's rage and his defense abilities complement Rappa's attack skills. His Barrier Quirk creates an impenetrable shield that is hard to break through, making him a valuable and effective member of the Eight Bullets within the Shie Hassaikai.

DYNAMIC DEFENSE

During Rappa's battle with Fatgum and Kirishima, Tengai creates a shield to protect him from their blows. After the Shie Hassaikai raid, Tengai is taken to prison with the rest of his gang.

DID YOU KNOW?

Tengai is very obedient and always follows Overhaul's orders.

BIRTHDAY: *Unknown*
HEIGHT: *Unknown*
QUIRK: *Barrier*
AFFILIATION: *Shie Hassaikai*
QUOTE: *"My duty is to rein you from running unbridled."*

Shin Nemoto

A gang member who always gets to the truth

Nemoto is a loyal member of the Shie Hassaikai and devoted to its leader, Overhaul. His Confession Quirk enables him to ask any question and get a truthful answer. Overhaul trusts Nemoto, one of the Eight Bullets, and shares his plans for the future with him.

SHOOTS TO KILL

When the Pro Heroes invade Shie Hassaikai's HQ, Nemoto selflessly fights back and shoots at Togata to give his boss Overhaul time to escape.

DID YOU KNOW?

Sometimes his Quirk brings out the truth even his victims didn't know.

BIRTHDAY: *Unknown*
HEIGHT: *Unknown*
QUIRK: *Confession*
AFFILIATION: *Shie Hassaikai*
QUOTE: *"Did Shigaraki ever mention that he'd betray us?"*

Gentle Criminal

The well-mannered villain who loves to go viral

An internet sensation, Gentle Criminal hungers for fame and broadcasts his criminal acts online to gain popularity. He uses his Elasticity Quirk to make anything he touches stretchy and bouncy—a useful skill for escaping crime scenes in a hurry.

PARTNERS IN CRIME

After Gentle Criminal commits his crimes, his sidekick La Brava shares videos of them online. He plans to infiltrate U.A. High School's Festival, hoping to be the center of attention, but is forced to flee when Midoriya tries to stop him.

BIRTHDAY: *August 29*
HEIGHT: *181 cm (5 ft 11 in)*
QUIRK: *Elasticity*
AFFILIATION: *Villain*
QUOTE: *"The romance of a curious genius is unleashed."*

DID YOU KNOW?

Gentle Criminal can make the air elastic and uses it like a trampoline to bounce around on.

La Brava

The tech expert who will do anything for love

La Brava loves and admires Gentle Criminal and devotes herself to promoting him online using her excellent computer skills. She is happy to break the law if it helps Gentle Criminal in any way. Her Love Quirk enables her to give anyone she loves a power boost. The more she loves them, the more powerful the boost is.

THE POWER OF LOVE

La Brava is outraged when Midoriya uses his Delaware Smash Air Force move on her beloved Gentle Criminal. She helps Gentle Criminal escape by giving him a power boost with her Love Quirk.

DID YOU KNOW?
She can activate her Quirk only once a day.

BIRTHDAY: *February 14*
HEIGHT: *111 cm (3 ft 8 in)*
QUIRK: *Love*
AFFILIATION: *Villain*
QUOTE: *"This plan is failing, so we must retreat."*

Re-Destro

The mastermind intent on destroying hero society

As grand commander of the Meta Liberation Army, Re-Destro has the Meta Ability (his name for Quirk) Stress, which he uses to convert stress into power. The more stress he experiences, the stronger he becomes. He's also the CEO of the Detnerat company that seemingly supports the hero industry but actually seeks to destroy it.

He is always seen in a pinstripe suit with green shirt and tie

A dark, fire-shaped stain around his eyes creates a mask when he's upset

DID YOU KNOW?
Re-Destro is arrested after being defeated in battle by Edge Shot.

NEW LEADER

When Re-Destro loses in combat to Tomura Shigaraki in Deika City, he tells him that the Meta Liberation Army is his to command and that he can carry on his mission of liberating society.

BIRTHDAY: *Unknown*
HEIGHT: *Unknown*
QUIRK: *Stress*
AFFILIATION: *Meta Liberation Army*
QUOTE: *"Our objective is to liberate all Metahumans."*

Skeptic

A strategic puppet master who shapes the media

The intelligent strategist for the Meta Liberation Army, Skeptic has the Meta Ability Anthropomorph. He is able to transform and control objects, making them move as he wishes. His intelligence makes him very useful to the army and a dangerous enemy to everyone else.

TECH GENIUS

Skeptic's computer skills are a vital propaganda tool for The Paranormal Liberation Army. He also uses his laptop to spy on others and control the puppets he creates with his Quirk.

Long, jet-black hair swirls around his head

DID YOU KNOW?

Skeptic wanted to kill Himiko Toga and let Twice join the Meta Liberation Army for his Double Quirk.

BIRTHDAY: *Unknown*
HEIGHT: *Unknown*
AFFILIATION: *Meta Liberation Army*
QUIRK: *Anthropomorph*
QUOTE: *"This is all to plan! I'm just prepping for my next move."*

Trumpet

The silver-tongued politician with big ambitions

Party leader and commander in the Meta Liberation Army, Trumpet has the Meta Ability Incite. The electromagnetic waves in his voice, along with his skill at public speaking, help him manipulate supporters and get others to do what he wants.

DID YOU KNOW?
Trumpet becomes one of the nine lieutenants of the Paranormal Liberation Front.

PARTY STARTER

Trumpet and Curious are sent by Re-Destro to meet with Tomura Shigaraki. He cordially invites the villains to join them for a revival party before beginning the attack.

BIRTHDAY: *Unknown*
HEIGHT: *Unknown*
QUIRK: *Incite*
AFFILIATION: *Meta Liberation Army*
QUOTE *"Welcome in, new friends, to our Revival Party."*

Geten

A cool, cunning ice villain dedicated to the cause

A loyal member of the Meta Liberation Army, Geten has a cunning strategy for every battle. His Ice Manipulation Meta Ability enables him to shape and manipulate ice with chilling consequences. After his Quirk awakening, he is able to alter the temperature of water, enabling him to transform any water in his radius into his icy weapons.

DID YOU KNOW?
Geten never attended school but has spent his life learning to control his icy ability.

BIRTHDAY: *Unknown*
HEIGHT: *Unknown*
QUIRK: *Ice Manipulation*
AFFILIATION: *Meta Liberation Army*
QUOTE: *"There's more to my ability than simple manipulation."*

Blue coat with a fur-trim collar

Beige, knee-high boots

ICE-COOL COMBAT

When Re-Destro declares war on the League of Villains, Geten channels his powerful ice weapons at Dabi and manages to destroy part of Twice's clone army.

Curious

The explosive villain who loves playing with fire

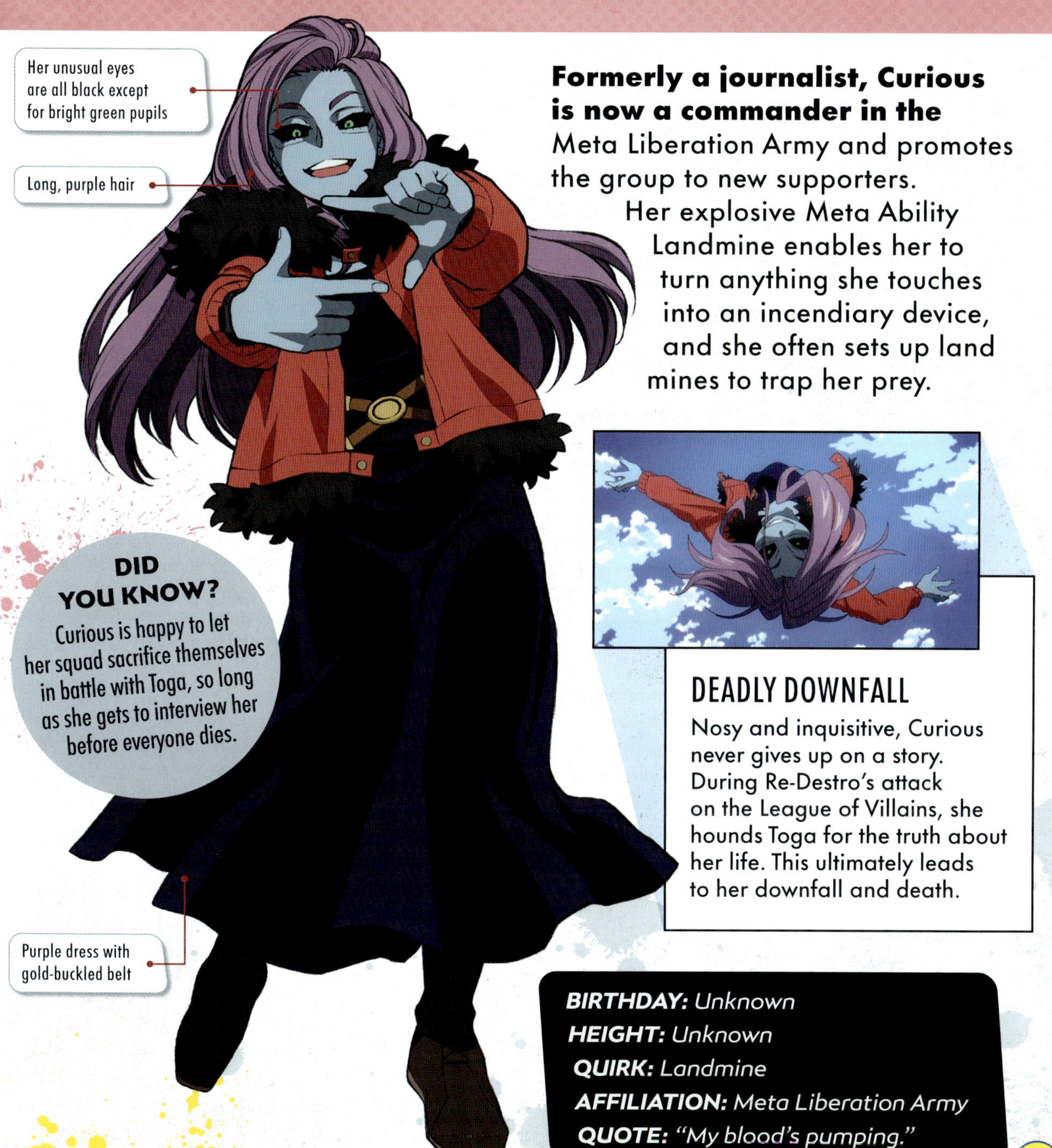

Formerly a journalist, Curious is now a commander in the Meta Liberation Army and promotes the group to new supporters. Her explosive Meta Ability Landmine enables her to turn anything she touches into an incendiary device, and she often sets up land mines to trap her prey.

DID YOU KNOW?

Curious is happy to let her squad sacrifice themselves in battle with Toga, so long as she gets to interview her before everyone dies.

DEADLY DOWNFALL

Nosy and inquisitive, Curious never gives up on a story. During Re-Destro's attack on the League of Villains, she hounds Toga for the truth about her life. This ultimately leads to her downfall and death.

BIRTHDAY: *Unknown*
HEIGHT: *Unknown*
QUIRK: *Landmine*
AFFILIATION: *Meta Liberation Army*
QUOTE: *"My blood's pumping."*